FISH & CHIP SHOPS

England's top 100 fish and chip shops

Tony Mudd

foreword by William Black

G000116760

studio **cactus**

First published in Great Britain in 2002 by

studio **cactus** ltd

13 SOUTHGATE STREET WINCHESTER HAMPSHIRE SO23 9DZ
TEL 01962 878600 FAX 01962 850209 ISDN 01962 859277
E-MAIL MAIL@STUDIOCACTUS.CO.UK WEBSITE WWW.STUDIOCACTUS.CO.UK

Thanks to Hodder Headline for permission to use extracts
from *Fish!* by S. Grigson and W. Black, Headline, 1998; and
A Lot of Hard Yakka by S. Hughes, Headline 2000; and to
Allison and Busby Ltd for permission to use the extract from
Collected Poems 1967–85, A. Henri, 1986.

A catalogue record for this book is
available from the British Library.

Reproduced, printed and bound by
L&S Printing Group, UK

Contents

Foreword

It wasn't that long ago – in the middle of the 19th century – that the sacred tradition of frying fish started. Originally, fish and chips (the chips came later it seems) were a street food, and in a sense there they have remained. To many people they will always taste infinitely better wrapped in an obscure local newspaper that will tell you all about WI meetings and flower displays in the village hall.

What is essentially a marvellously simple way of cooking fish – frying – seals in the flavour perfectly if cooked correctly: temperature, the quality of the cooking oil and the freshness of the fish must all be just right. It also helps to find a good fishmonger and encourage him or her to find you the best and the freshest fish around.

What about the batter? There are many variations and the choice must largely be a matter of personal taste. Whether you use beer or matzo meal, fish and chips need good batter and good oil, or the best dripping, to fry it all in.

It may sound simple, but as practically everyone in this book will tell you, it isn't! And then there are all the extras. The tartare sauce, the mushy peas, the vinegar... and don't forget the saveloys, the faggots or the meat pies.

Mmmmmm.... The smell will soon be wafting from these very pages!

Deep-fried battered haddock

Taken from *Fish* by Sophie Grigson and William Black, published by Headline

Here's one half of the most famous, widely eaten British fish speciality, good old fish and chips. It's not much hassle to turn your kitchen into the local chippy for an evening: I reckon you can probably manage your own chips, so here is a recipe for their partner, deep-fried fish in a crisp batter. Made with really fresh fish and eaten hot from the pan, it is a dish to be proud of. I love deep-fried haddock, but all manner of fish take well to the chip-shop approach. Whatever you use, make sure it is really fresh and you instantly lift your battered fish above the average offering. Serve it with tartare sauce or wedges of lemon, or tomato ketchup or vinegar – whatever takes your fancy (and chips, of course).

Serves 4

oil or dripping for deep-frying

4 skinned haddock fillets, weighing about 175g (6oz) each

lemon wedges, tartare sauce, malt vinegar and/or tomato ketchup, to serve

For the batter:

225g (8oz) plain flour, sifted

300ml (½ pint) lager or brown ale

1 egg, separated

1 tablespoon sunflower oil

110ml (4 fl oz) water

salt and pepper

To make the batter, season the flour with salt and pepper. Make a well in the centre and add the lager, egg yolk and oil. Gradually whisk into the flour to make a smooth batter. Stir in the water. Leave to rest for at least half an hour. Shortly before using, whisk the egg white until it forms stiff peaks and fold into the batter.

Heat the oil to 180°C/350°F, or until a cube of bread dropped into it sizzles fairly vigorously straight away. One by one, dry the haddock pieces. Then dip into the batter, making sure that they are completely coated. Slide into the oil and fry for about 5–6 minutes, depending on the thickness of the fish, until golden brown. Drain briefly on kitchen paper and sprinkle with salt. Eat immediately.

William Black, Food Writer

Author's introduction

When I came up with the idea for this book I had an inkling of the passion surrounding the subject, but what I didn't count on was the sheer strength of feeling. Fish and chips are so much a part of the English landscape that it is easy to take them for granted, yet everyone has an opinion about them.

In this book I have put together a selection of the best fish and chip shops and restaurants in the country and I've done this by asking you – the paying and eating public – to recommend them to me. During the research I've been interviewed on most local radio stations and I've asked listeners to nominate their favourite shops, which I have then visited in order to pick out the best. This is a subjective guide, so if your own favourite is missing, contact me through the publishers (by email or letter; see details opposite) and I shall consider it for the second edition. (Please note that I have listed each shop by the name it is known by – this sometimes differs from that on the shopfront.)

6

By way of apology to those living in Scotland, Wales and Ireland (where I know they have great fish and chips), let me explain that merely for the sake of simplicity did we choose to begin with a guide to England's best fish and chips. However, we intend to include the best shops and restaurants that you recommend for your regions in the second edition, thus expanding the book.

Finally, I have found researching this book an absolute pleasure, not only because of the great fish and chips I've sampled but also because of the many interesting, hospitable and downright pleasant people it has given me the chance to meet. I've also heard some great stories, and discovered the ins and outs of a fascinating business that, unjustifiably, has been virtually ignored for years in this country but which is an intrinsic part of it. I think I have also discovered the answer to what makes the best fish and chip shops – it's the people who run them. The owners and fryers of the finest shops love what they do, so everything else falls into place. The work is hardly worth doing simply for the kind of money they earn (they work too hard and for too many hours to justify that). So I hope you'll enjoy the fruits of my labours and that they will prompt you to get out there and try somewhere new. Remember, too, that if you find a great shop that does not appear in the book, we want to know about it (it must offer a takeaway service).

Tony Mudd

Contact us at:

studio cactus ltd

13 SOUTHGATE STREET   WINCHESTER   HAMPSHIRE   SO23 9DZ

E-MAIL: MAIL@STUDIOCACTUS.CO.UK

www.tiptopguides.co.uk

Healthy eating

A meal of fish and chips provides iron, calcium, fat, protein and energy – all necessary to keep you ticking along efficiently. Fish ranks among the most nutritious of all foods, containing the same levels of protein as meat yet demanding little energy to digest it. Potatoes, on the other hand, contain minerals, carbohydrate and vitamins.

Since the fish is sealed in batter it steams inside it, emerging from the pans virtually fat-free (by which I mean 90–95% free of fat). In fact, on average, a fish and chip supper contains less fat than either a curry or a burger. No wonder doctors have recommended a regular meal of fish and chips to pregnant women.

History
The beginnings

As the Industrial Revolution gathered pace in the England of the 18th and 19th centuries, it brought with it extraordinary economic and trade expansion. In the ports and industrial towns and in London's East End, street traders already sold fried fish as one dish (originally a Middle-Eastern idea), cooked potatoes as another.

The big debate is about whether the first fish-and-potato meal was sold in London or Lancashire, and whether it was, indeed, this combination of foods that spawned the first fish and chip shop. No matter where the beginnings, fish and chip shops were soon spreading like wildfire as families started their own businesses in their front rooms.

Today's fish and chip shops

Most of the shops that I've picked out for this book are still traditional community fish and chip shops for which the passing tourist trade provides an added bonus. They offer a service to regular patrons and form a part of the glue of society, just like the pub, the butcher's, the newsagent's and the bookie's. During both World Wars, fish and chips helped to feed the masses. In fact, during the Second World War, the only takeaway food not to be rationed was fish and chips, and mobile vans were used to transport the food to evacuees around the country. Some people may consider fish and chips to be relics of a bygone age, but in fact they represent something quintessentially, and eccentrically, English.

Joseph Carney sells fish from his barrow at Seven Dials, London **1877**

Any chip shop queue around the country reflects all races and creeds wanting the same thing – good hot food that doesn't look or taste like it has been produced by some poor soul with a forced smile and a few set lines to say.

Lately, people have been asking what it means to be English – or British. If you're having problems defining your cultural identity, queue up for some fish and chips. It'll soon come back to you.

Customers outside a fish and chip shop
circa 1934

How do you like your fish & chips?

Fresh fish or frozen at sea?

This really is a tough one. There is, of course, no argument against fresh fish – it looks and tastes great. Good quality fresh fish, eaten within one to two days of being caught is going to be delicious. But it's not easy to obtain fish this fresh and, sometimes, things are different – the fish has been kept on ice on the boat for a couple of days before being delivered to the market and from there to the supplier, who delivers to the fish shop. So how fresh is it by this time? Well, the answer is it's still fresh enough to taste good. Any longer, though, and it starts to lose its attraction. The sort of fish you want should have white flesh once cooked – in other words, as soon as it starts to lose its whiteness, it has been lying about for too long.

The next best alternative is to use fish that was frozen on the very day it was caught at sea, in factory ships or in a freezer in the ship's hold. Once frozen, it will retain its vibrant taste and be easier to keep. Its flavour will also be consistent once cooked.

Top or tail?

You might think that, given the choice, most people would opt for the thick, succulent top end of the fish. However, it is actually the tail end that is known as "the fishmonger's choice" because it is free of bones. In a good chippy you shouldn't have to worry about bones, but if you're feeding the kids and want to be sure, insist on a tail.

Skin on or skin off?

Why do some people like skin on one side of their battered fried fish and others prefer none at all? Some feel that the skin helps to prevent the fish from drying out during the cooking process, and that it heightens the flavour. Others find the skin completely unpalatable. Your taste probably depends upon where you were brought up. As a general rule, people living on the east coast of England and in the Home Counties prefer the skin on, but those on the west coast from Devon to Cumbria generally prefer the skin off. However, a hard-and-fast dividing line between east and west does not exist – for example, some Yorkshire shops serve fish with the skin off and some Lancastrian ones with the skin on. On the other hand, in the Midlands the divide is indeed roughly east-west, but here and there you'll find shops serving fish without its skin in otherwise skin-on counties, and vice versa. As for London, well it's mostly skin on – except where it's skin off…

Frying in beef dripping or oil?

What do you like to have your fish and chips fried in? The people of Yorkshire seem to prefer beef dripping, while Lancastrians favour either groundnut oil or palm oil. However, when I was in Yorkshire, many a chippy told me about the number of Lancastrians who cross the border for the taste of traditional beef dripping; yet plenty of Yorkshiremen cross in the other direction in order to avoid it.

Technically, the end result is not much affected by whether it was fried in oil or fat, so your choice is dictated by other concerns. It just depends on what you are used to and what you like or are health-conscious about (although if fish and chips are cooked properly they absorb little fat or oil and are a healthy contribution to a balanced diet). Vegetarians also want to be sure that their chips are not fried in beef dripping.

All oils can burn and if you've ever found that the taste of a fish-and-chip meal has repeated on you for a few hours, it's because the oil has burned and the carbon fragments have been left in it. In a good shop this does not happen and the oil is filtered.

Lastly of course there is temperature. The aim is to quickly seal the fish in the batter so that it can steam inside its coating – high heat is best.

John Prescott, Deputy Leader of the Labour Party, enjoying fish and chips in Cleethorpes **1996**

The batter

At first glance, batter seems such a simple thing, but I'm amazed at the variety of recipes, as well as methods of storing and using it.

The basic batter mixture is usually pretty standard. But, having said that, other ingredients can be added. For example, you can add vinegar or yeast; you can make a kosher batter with matzo-meal flour; or, to make a tempura (light Japanese) batter, you can use only flour, water and salt, replacing tap water with carbonated mineral water or soda water. Most fish and chip shops use a standard batter mixture, although

Many shops have their own variation on the standard batter

14

many like to add some of their own ingredients. Some shops keep the details of their own personal batter recipe a closely-guarded secret.

Should the batter be golden? I must say that I like a pale gold version that is crisp to bite and slightly dry on the inside but sealing succulent fish. If the batter is oily or soggy it won't have done its job properly.

Finally, it's worth remembering one school of thought that suggests that the batter's sole purpose is to seal the fish so that it can cook inside, and that you're not supposed to eat it at all.

The spuds

The potato was first brought to this country by Sir Walter Raleigh in Elizabethan times and has been a staple food ever since. Today, we can choose between hundreds of varieties, many suitable for chips. However, most fish and chip shops favour the Maris Piper, which makes a great chip, has a low sugar content so it doesn't turn dark before the chips are cooked, and benefits from a guaranteed supply at an acceptable price. In this book, 90 per cent of the shops use Maris Piper, so unless stated otherwise, you can assume that this is what you are getting.

Over the years, potato crops have gone up and down and crops that are not grown in such abundance as Maris Pipers find it virtually impossible to compete. However, King Edwards make great chips, as do Pink Fir Apple and Desirée, to name but a few.

Usually the less successful chips appear in the summer when the old spuds are replaced by the new ones for about three weeks around July. The new potatoes have a higher water content, making it difficult to produce a chip that's crisp on the outside and fluffy inside.

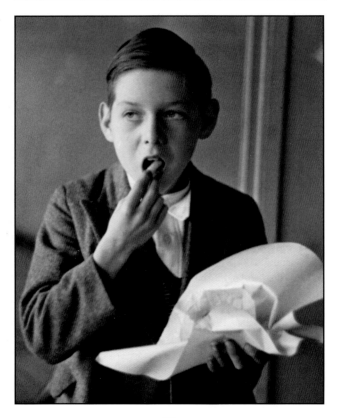

Chips – thick, thin or medium?

Let me say from the start that thin chips are a travesty. I hate thin chips for several reasons. They absorb too much oil, can't retain the heat and taste like cardboard. Added to that the fast-food versions are not made entirely of potato. A good chip has to be at least 12mm thick so that it will cook properly and retain much of its goodness and flavour. Thicker chips are generally more popular in the north of the country and medium chips in the south. Good fish and chip shops never serve the thin ones.

Gravy or gherkins?

I have restricted myself to mentioning only the extras that I found to be particularly tasty or special in some way. Once again, we find a north-south divide in customer preference. Northerners, for example, enjoy gravy with their chips, while the young all over the country favour curry sauce. Mushy peas are popular with young and old alike, but most prevalent in the north. Baked beans are for children; and pickles (especially onions and gherkins) sell best south of the Watford Gap. I'm a southerner by birth but I think mushy peas go superbly with fish and chips, adding colour, texture and nutrition (by the way, with mint added you get "posh mushys") and from time to time I also enjoy a wallie (a pickled gherkin that apparently originated in eastern Europe). These days, many shops offer a slice of lemon with the fish, which is a bit redundant if you're using vinegar or tartare sauce (the latter particularly tasty if home-made). Other popular side orders include mayonnaise and coleslaw.

17

The Seafish Friers Quality Award

Shops holding the Seafish Friers Quality Award are nationally recognized for producing first-class fish and chips in a first-class environment.

The Award scheme was started in 1996 with the aim of raising standards within the fish-frying trade, enhancing the profile of the industry and promoting customer loyalty to both the product and individual Award-holding shops.

The Sea Fish Industry Authority, set up by Act of Parliament to support and develop the UK Fish Industry, is responsible for the management and authorization of the Award. Assessments are carried out by Seafish Approved Inspectors who are highly trained professionals.

Identifying Award holders

An Award-holding shop displays the logo (shown above) in the form of a window sticker, poster, sign or light box, and a certificate. The certificate and window sticker are dated with the year in which the shop achieved the Award.

How shops achieve the Award

After applying to the Sea Fish Industry Authority, a thorough inspection assesses the shop's image, design and condition; selection and quality of raw materials; storage practices; hygiene; product handling and temperature control; product wrapping; staff training; equipment; frying and sales skills; and, most importantly, the quality of the final cooked product.

The Award is valid for one year and its retention depends on the high standards being maintained. The Seafish Approved Inspectors reserve the right to visit the shops unannounced at any time and, if the standards have fallen, the Award can be withdrawn.

Quality Award-holding fish and chip shops

Seafish Friers Quality Award holders are highlighted in this book by the Award logo. The current full list of Award-holding fish and chip shops in England is at the back of this book. The list can also be found on the Seafish website: www.seafish.co.uk

---

Symbols used in this book

B Cooked in beef fat

V Cooked in vegetable oil

S Cooked with the skin on

S̸ Cooked with the skin off

If, for example, the "skin on" symbol is qualified by "except cod", this means all fish is served skin on, apart from cod (which is served skin off).
If both beef fat and vegetable oil symbols are shown, a mix of the two is used.

|O| Restaurant   **Y** Licensed restaurant   **BH** Open on bank holidays

---

"Love is fish and chips on winter nights"

Adrian Henri (Liverpool poet)

Extract from the poem *Love is...*
(*Collected Poems 1967–85*)

The
North

Carlo's

7–9 Market Street, Alnwick, Northumberland
Mon–Fri 11.30am–2.30pm/4.30–10.30pm, Sat 11.30am–10pm • Busiest Fri, Sat and Easter–Sept

In parts, Northumberland is unspoiled, owning a magnificent coastline and some delightfully underpopulated and extremely pretty towns, as well as some tremendous historic sights and buildings. A perfect example of this is the little town of Alnwick, with its cobbled streets and charming market square that brims with stalls on Thursday and Saturday, while a farmers'

market is held on the last Friday of every month.

Just 20 metres away from the town square, Carlo's also looks pretty impressive – a successful conversion of two shops with large bay windows that allow plenty of light in.

Is fish really good for the brain? Well, TV's celebrated brainbox Car Vorderman is a big fish and chip fan. She says, "There's magic in

The place has been run by Laura and Carlo Biagioni for the last 12 years.

The shop's gleaming takeaway counter is fronted by an airy restaurant. Both the shop and restaurant have a fast and efficient air, but you never feel rushed and Carlo seems to know most of his customers' names, together with their usual orders.

The main attraction is cod from Norwegian and Icelandic waters, followed, to a lesser degree, by haddock and plaice. The fish is generously portioned and boned on the premises. The Biagionis make their own batter and coat the fish in rice flour before dipping it in the creamy mix and frying it at 180°C. The thick chips are cooked at 145°C, and the mushy peas get an overnight soaking and come up a vibrant green with a pleasing gloopy consistency. If you want to eat outside you probably won't find a much better place than the benches near the clocktower just over the road.

late of fish and chips. As a child I had it three or four times week …". What more proof do you need?

Charlies

Albert Street, Amble, Morpeth, Northumberland
Mon–Wed 4.30–9pm, Thurs–Sat 11.30am–9pm, Sun 4.30–9pm • Busiest on Friday

B **S**

Amble may not look like much when you first drive in, especially if you're approaching from the south, past the collieries further down the coast. However it's rather a pleasing little tourist town with a narrow, pedestrianized and pretty high street.

The town's best fish and chip shop is on the way in to the high street – amid some rather squat pre-Second-World-War

terraced housing on the main road. For 16 years, it has been owned and run by the delightful Charlie and Joyce Willoughby. He used to be a taxi driver, she a teacher, and when they bought the place (using every last penny they

Assuming you choose not to eat in the intimate street-fron restaurant, you can take your pick of plenty of eating spo

had) they had not fried a single fish in their lives. To help, the previous owner offered to stay for a week and teach them the ropes, but promptly reneged on the agreement, so they were left  frying fish for the first time on their first night. Bravely they asked each customer on that fateful evening to tell them what they were doing wrong and what they were doing right and as the weeks passed, they gradually refined their technique.

At Charlies they use only the best cod, haddock and plaice that they can find (which is usually from Iceland), and portion it on the premises into three sizes – 6oz, 8oz and 10oz. The fish is boned, served with the skin on and dipped in a simple batter mix that comes up light and thin with a good rich colour. The chips are cut to a medium thickness, blanched and then flash-fried to finish them off, and everything is cooked in beef dripping at about 180°C.

with a view within a couple of minutes' drive. My favourite is down y the river estuary overlooking the harbour.

Balls of Prudhoe

39 Front Street, Prudhoe, Northumberland
Mon/Tues 3.30pm–midnight, Wed/Thurs 11am–2pm/3.30pm–midnight, Fri/Sat 11am–midnight

V **S** cod **S** haddock

Prudhoe is a small, quiet hillside community just outside Newcastle-upon-Tyne and not far from part of Hadrian's Wall. The shop is run by Ann, who took it over from her mum and dad, but the story of how they came to own it is quite amazing. Ann's mother had worked in the shop as an assistant for the previous owners and one day they asked her if she wanted to buy the place. Her boss explained that the reason he was selling was that, according to his religion, the world was about to end!

The main draws here are cod and haddock, dipped in home-made batter to create a light dry finish, with the fish melting in your mouth.

Regular customers here have their fish fried for exactly the right amount of time to suit their individual tastes.

Bill's Fish Bar

4a Victoria Crescent, Cullercoats, North Shields/Newcastle-upon-Tyne, Tyne and Wear
Daily from 11.30am–9.30pm; closed only on Christmas Day • Busiest weekends and evenings

Perched on a road that tops a horseshoe-shaped bay, Bill's Fish Bar is no more than 50 metres from the sea, and its first-floor restaurant commands a spectacular view.
Bill gets most of his fish locally and concentrates on cod and haddock, coated in an ingenious batter (made using a standard mix plus vinegar), which enhances the flavours. Everything comes in big portions,

including the thick chips, the home-made mushy peas, the gravy and the curry sauce. Visitors and locals alike are assured of a hearty welcome. That's probably why the TV and movie star Jimmy Nail sometimes calls in for a bite.

here is an added bonus for pensioners who eat at this restaurant:
a and bread and butter, at no extra cost.

Kristian Fish Company

2–5 Union Quay, North Shields Fish Quay, Newcastle-upon-Tyne, Tyne and Wear
Mon–Sat 11am–9pm, Sun 11.30am–4.30pm • Busiest Sun, summer evenings, winter lunchtimes

The other jewel in the Tyne and Wear crown is Kristian's, a thriving component in the small fish empire of the ever friendly Joe Stevenson – one-time trawler owner, fish wholesaler and monger. This bustling little takeaway is situated on a redeveloped old fish quay on the north bank of the River Tyne, against a backdrop of the south bank's defunct shipyards. Next door is a stylish and comfy restaurant. Many of the quay's old warehouses have been converted into flats and a large proportion of the once busy dockside is given over to retail outlets, cafés, restaurants and pubs – with the old chain-and-rope hoist beams still jutting out above the street. The area retains a hint of its original charm; a couple of fishing boats continue to use the docks, as indicated by the crab and lobster pots strewn around, while kids frequently rod-fish in the river.

Jack Charlton (1966 World Cup winner and former manager of Th
Republic of Ireland football team) was so impressed he left a £5 tip

Joe knows his fish, so the haddock or cod comes from as far afield as Peterhead or as close as Grimsby or Lowestoft, depending on where he can find the best. The fish is accompanied by good chunky chips and a choice of home-made curry sauce, gravy or mushy peas. The locals must have a high opinion of the end product, judging by the queues, and the fact that the *Newcastle Evening Chronicle* amusingly entitled a piece about the shop "Batter By Far".

The *Northern Echo* made the Kristian Fish Company "Chipper of the Year" in 1992.

Beedle's

2 Oaklea Terrace, Cockton Hill Road, Bishop Auckland, County Durham
Mon–Sat 11am–11.30pm • Busiest Friday 4–6.30pm

 haddock

Beedle's is easy to miss in a car, being tucked away on a tiny terraced street that is blocked off from the main road. Access is via St James Street, the next one along.

Peter Beedle has run the shop for ten years, although it has functioned as a chippy since 1920. It's a delightfully decorated corner takeaway of the old school where they serve mostly cod but also lemon sole, haddock and plaice, all from Iceland. The fish is portioned by hand, boned and dipped in a creamy home-made batter. It's fried at high temperatures to produce soft, steaming white fish and golden batter. The chips are thick, and inserted into butties to order. Specially designed boxes keep everything warm and carry a voucher to encourage people to return them rather than create litter. So this shop not only provides a top culinary treat but also aims to protect the environment.

The home-made mushy peas at Beedle's won a Batchelor award not so long ago and thus warrant a try.

Bell's Fish and Chip Shop

33 Marshall Terrace, Gilesgate Moor, Durham, County Durham
Mon–Thurs/Sat 11.15am–1.30pm/5–10pm, Fri 11.15am–10pm • Busiest weekends

Gilesgate Moor is just ten minutes' drive from the centre of Durham. Graham Kennedy has owned this shop for about six years and got involved in the business simply because his parents lived opposite a chippy.

He sells mainly cod from Iceland or Norway, and haddock from the Arctic. He portions his own fish and cuts a good-sized piece. The fish is battered in his own perfected recipe and fried in beef dripping, as are the thick chips. Graham makes his own mushy peas, plus a variety of other sauces. While you're in the shop, check out the huge and atmospheric painting by P. Bainbridge of a fisherman pulling in his nets during rough weather. You might also want to spare a thought for the ex-manager of Coventry Football Club, Gordon Strachan, who once came in and asked for sixteen portions to take on the bus home. Coventry must have lost again.

y Bell's great-value "Fish and Chip Buttie" – two standard ieces of fish plus a large roll filled with chips for £1.50.

Morleys

12 Fore Bondgate, Bishop Auckland, County Durham
Mon–Wed 11.30am–1.30pm, Thurs–Fri 11am–2pm, Sat 11am–3pm • Busiest Thurs & Sat

You can't miss Morleys in the pedestrianized thoroughfare just 40 metres from the main market square, which holds a market on Tuesday and Saturday. The shop does a roaring trade during the day, but closes in the evenings (if you find yourself in need of evening fish and chips, head for Beedle's, p30).

For the last nine years, Morleys has been run by Elizabeth and David Ruffles, whose story is rather heart-warming. They realized one day that their children had flown the nest, but David still worked in Saudi Arabia for extended periods while Elizabeth pursued her career

The fish is often freshly fried to order, since they're so bus
that the hot box of their cooking range empties after a coup

in Bishop Auckland. Alarmed at the high rate of marriage breakdowns, they decided to start again by buying a fish and chip shop and running it together to avoid becoming just another divorce statistic. The tactic clearly worked, proof that fish and chips have a romance all of their own.

The shop's custom is mostly local and regular, enjoying chiefly cod and haddock from the Faroe Islands, which is filleted and portioned on the premises. The batter is light and the fish has a fluffy steak-like quality that melts in your mouth. The thickly cut chips are pre-fried and finished off with a flash-fry just before you get them in order to perk them up;

and their home-made mushy peas have an excellent reputation. For the enjoyment of your meal you'll find plenty of places to perch and people-watch round the market square.

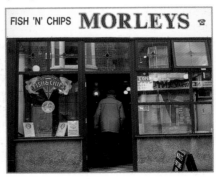

f minutes. At Morley's they live by the philosophy that "you can't uy a Mini at the back door and sell it as a Rolls at the front".

Stramongate Chip Shop

74 Stramongate, Kendal, Cumbria
Mon–Sat 11.30am–1.30pm/evenings (hours vary) • Busiest Friday 4.30–6.30pm

If you're looking for something a bit more substantial than a hunk of Kendal mint cake, you'll find a wonderful little chippy near the footbridge over the picturesque River Kent, and just down the hill from the mazey mixture of "yards" and "ginnels" that branch off the attractive and historic high street of Kendal. Although advertised as a "gateway to the Lakes", the town is, in fact, a considerable distance from Windermere and the Lakes proper, but well worth a visit for all that.

This bright and simple shop is situated on the ground floor of a tall, narrow house, and

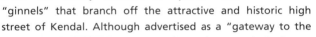

has been operated for the last 18 years by Eric and Lynda Leigh, although between them and their forebears they have at least 39 years' experience. The haddock (one of their biggest sellers) comes from the North Sea, while the cod (also a big favourite) is Icelandic. Both are served with the skin off and boned,

having been cut into pretty generous pieces in the shop.

The whiteboard behind the counter announces any other fish on offer, or special deals for the day. Eric and Lynda coat their fish in a batter that is beaten until it's bubbly and fry it in pure vegetable oil at about 190°C, which steams the fish and gives the batter a crisp finish. They also make a thick chip here and their own glorious mushy peas.

This shop has a loyal following of locals and out-of-towners alike. Additionally, Stramongate does a great deal of work for local charities and, despite the tourist influx for six months of the year, this is a truly traditional community shop.

Patrick Moore CBE says, "I am definitely a fish-and-chip enthusiast. I always prefer eating things that come out of the sea ...".

Matties

186 Ainslie Street, Barrow-in-Furness, Cumbria
Mon–Sat 11.30am–2pm/4.30–9pm • Busiest Thurs, Fri and Sat lunchtime and teatime

Barrow-in-Furness is lucky enough to have one of the friendliest fish and chip shops I've ever visited. Mattie and Marilyn Bull have worked in the business for 39 years and plan to continue for a long time to come.

The dominant fish at Matties is haddock (and we're talking sit-up-and-take-notice flavour), followed by cod and plaice, all of which are delivered fresh from

Aberdeen. They cut a thick chip and produce a tasty green mass of mushy peas. The sea is about ten minutes' drive away, but you can opt instead for the peace and quiet of a big tree-filled park five minutes (by car) up the road.

Matties has "never compromised on the price of raw material or the desire to create a good-value-for-money meal".

Townhead Chippy

46 Stricklandgate, Penrith, Cumbria

Mon–Fri 11.30am–1.30pm/4.30–10pm, Sat 11.30am–2pm/4.30–10pm, Sun 4–9.30pm • Busiest Fri

Penrith has two first-class fish and chip shops, one a takeaway (described here), the other a restaurant and walk-in counter (Scott's, p38). The Townhead Chippy is run by Huw and Julia Gruffydd, who have owned the shop for about two years. The shop itself has existed for over 80 years and originally boasted a coal-fired range (now in York Museum). Cod is king, ruling over haddock and

plaice, all from the Bering Sea. The fish is portioned on the premises, to a standard size of about 5oz or, for a larger piece, 7oz. As well as mushy peas they stock impressive steak-and-kidney and mince-and-onion pies.

They cut thick chips at the Townhead, believing "you're always recommended on the quality of your chips".

Scott's

Sandgate, Penrith, Cumbria
Mon–Sat 11.30am–2pm/evenings from 4.30pm • Busiest weekends and market days (Tues/Sat)

V ∅   Ⴈ ⅠⓄⅠ

The second (only in number) of the glorious two in Penrith, and a very different cup of tea from its competition just up the road (see Townhead Chippy, p37) is Scott's, situated on the corner of what looks like a small village square, in front of a big shopping arcade and historic church. The restaurant is an air-cooled, relaxing 50-seater where you can get anything from a chip buttie to a salmon steak, and the takeaway is a little corridor of hectic activity alongside it.

David Scott has operated the shop for eight years, and worked as a fishmonger before that, trying his hand as a buyer and frier. He's something of a perfectionist, experimenting with different frying methods and cooking ranges in an effort to get better and better at a job he obviously cares about deeply. In both the restaurant and shop they serve haddock

Naturally enough, the shop's main business comes from lip-smacking locals, but among other more occasional visitors is the

(predominantly), cod, plaice, halibut, hake, skate wings and salmon steak. The haddock is fresh from Aberdeen and most of the cod comes from the Norwegian fleet, and is portioned in the shop into big pieces and served with the skin off and the bones removed. Once dipped in a well-worked batter, the fish is fried in groundnut oil at somewhere between 170 and 175°C. David believes that if you fry at higher temperatures you burn the oil and introduce other, unwanted, tastes into the mix. The chips are thick and wholesome and the home-made mushy peas contain an extra touch of mint, which makes them both "posh" and especially tasty. When looking for somewhere to eat outside, you could try the leafy shade of the churchyard, which is no more than 50 metres away.

internationally renowned actor Tom Courtenay, who gives the place an extra bit of northern class.

Brian's

25 Gisburn Road, Hessle, East Yorkshire
Tues–Wed 4.30–6pm, Thurs 4.30–7pm, Fri 11.30am–1.30pm/4–7pm, Sat 11.30am–1.30pm

B **S**

In the shadow of the Humber Bridge and just to the west of Hull, lies the suburban settlement of Hessle. Brian's is about ten minutes' walk from the town square.

Hull's most famous resident – the talented, idiosyncratic and malcontent poet, Philip Larkin – would have approved of the rather curious opening times that Brian imposes upon the shop. But this system reflects the kind of shop he runs, as well as the regularity of its custom.

The most popular fish in the area is haddock, locally bought, but cod, skate and plaice are also available here if you prefer. Brian also produces delicious home-made fish cakes.

One of the best spots to munch your fare is just five minutes' drive away at the Humber Bridge viewpoint car park on Feriby Road.

Lead Lane

27–29 Lead Lane, Ripon, Yorkshire
Tues–Fri 11.30am–1.30pm/4.30–9pm, Sat 11.30am–1.30pm/4.30–8pm • Busiest Friday 4.30–6.30pm

Ripon is a pretty market town with the kind of unassuming character that means you have to delve to unearth its treasures. If you're prepared to go hunting further afield there are two good fish and chip shops, both a five-minute drive from the centre.

The Lead Lane chippy has a simple shopfront, in a row of housing-estate shops on the way into a large residential area. The shop has been run by Ray Boulding since 1994 and represents a radical departure for him from the computer industry in which he once earned his living. His cod comes from a variety of sources, but the haddock is fresh from Ireland and has a wonderful firm texture and distinctive flavour. The fish is dipped in his own special batter mix, before being fried at around 170°C. Ray cuts a medium chip and makes well-soaked mushy peas. Everything is wrapped in paper to take away.

Regulars wave at Ray on their way to the other shops and he starts their order so it's ready for their return.

41

Riverside

3a Church Street, Whitby, Yorkshire

Tues–Thurs 4.30–10pm, Fri–Sat 11.30am–1.30pm/4.30–10pm, Sun 4.30–10pm • Busiest eves/weekends

Whitby is probably best known for its immortalization in Bram Stoker's 1897 Gothic-horror novel, *Dracula*. Today, it is a popular tourist spot. The picturesque river-front bay, with its harbour, quays and fish piers, is littered with stalls, restaurants and shops offering meals of varying quality. But for the best food in town, head inland to the excellent Riverside.

Here you'll find a no-fuss shop run for the last 11 years by Mr Whittle, who has been buying, frying and selling fish for over 30 years. He serves local fresh fish (mostly haddock and cod), which is skinned and boned, cooked in a standard crisp batter, and accompanied by chunky chips.

On a fine day, a five-minute stroll will put you on a bench overlooking the river and its trawlers, inshore fishing boats, and lobster and crab pots.

Twice a year, there is a Goth day, when an army of would-be Transylvanians descends on Whitby in commemoration of Dracula.

Audrey's

2 Queen Street, Bridlington, Yorkshire
Daily 11.30am–6pm, school summer holidays 11.30am–9pm • Busiest weekends

B **S**

🍽️

Bridlington is a down-to-earth seaside resort laying claim to a long and engaging history. The best of a plethora of fish and chip shops in the town is undoubtedly Audrey's, owned by Mr Morrison, which is a cheery place with a comfortable restaurant on the floor above. The fish – mostly cod and haddock – is fresh from the local docks, apart from the plaice, which comes from further afield.

If you prefer to eat outside, a short walk from the shop through the alleyway on the other side of the road brings you to a path overlooking the harbour. There you'll find benches and hopeful anglers rod-fishing off the quayside.

Audrey's caters for a committed following of locals and passing trade from visitors who know a good thing when they see it.

Southgate Fisheries

36 Southgate, Ripon, Yorkshire

Mon–Sat 11.30am–1.15pm/evenings from 4.30pm • Busiest Friday afternoon and evening

B

Another excellent chippy in Ripon is the Southgate Fisheries. Helen James operates this well-groomed little shop. The main dishes are cod (from Iceland) and haddock (fresh from Aberdeen). The cod is cut into good-sized portions in-house to make a standard piece of 6oz; the haddock comes already cut, in impressive hunks. Helen uses a standard batter mix that she modifies to her own taste in order to get a very light finish. All the fish is cooked to order – except on Fridays when it's just too hectic – to ensure freshness. She cuts her chips quite thick and long, and par-fries them before giving them a flash-fry to finish them off. That way they end up crisp on the outside and still full of flavour on the inside. The mushy peas are reassuringly home-made, as are the excellent pea fritters; and the cooked food is wrapped in paper only.

Some of Helen's regulars on low-cholesterol diets are given fish so lightly battered there is barely any coating at all.

Dougies Fish & Chips

66 King Edward's Drive, Harrogate, Yorkshire

Mon/Tues 4.30–6.30pm, Wed–Sat 11.30am–1.30pm/evenings from 4.30pm • Busiest Friday evening

Just beyond the centre of Harrogate and about four minutes' drive on the Skipton Road is a residential area. Bang in the middle of this district is Doug Truscott's corner fish and chip shop. Doug has nearly 40 years'-worth of experience in the business and five in this shop and, as he says, "I don't do it because I want to make money; I do it because I love it".

The main attraction is cod, the other option being plaice. Doug portions the fish himself, a standard piece coming out on the hearty side of 6oz. Accompaniments include thick chips and excellent mushy peas.

About 90 per cent of the trade is local and 10 per cent passing tourists. Once visitors find the place, they tend to return.

"Of an evening, the home team minus Boycott retired to the Three Horseshoes up the Otley Road for a few pints of HDTs and a moan about Geoffrey. ('Why do people always take an instant dislike to me?' Boycott asked a colleague. 'Because it saves time', the player replied.) Then they directed the visitors to **Bryan's Fish Restaurant** next door. It's only in the Roses counties that places like this exist. Something between a Berni Inn and a canteen, it was stacked with togged up OAPs out for their Monday treat. They were served vast portions of crisply fried fish and chips, mushy peas, bread and butter, and pots of tea. **Even the baby haddock on the menu lapped over both sides of the plate.** The batter was light and crisp, not that saturated, chewy cardboard you get in most places, and the chips were perfect. Despite the fact that it was the best fried meal I had ever tasted, I couldn't finish mine. Gatting polished it off."

Simon Hughes (Author; Analyst for C4 cricket) *A Lot of Hard Yakka*

Bryan's

9 Weetwood Lane, Headingly, Leeds, Yorkshire

Mon–Sat midday–10pm, Sun midday–7pm (takeaway closes 30 mins later) • Busiest evenings

B **S**

Throughout Yorkshire, Bryan's is legendary. Originally a family business run by the Bryan family (from 1932), it was later bought by one of its regular customers, Jan Fletcher. Among the locals and others who travel regularly to the shop are Michael Parkinson and David Jason, as well as one visitor who came a very long way – from the White House in fact – Monica Lewinsky.

The most popular fish is haddock, but other options are fresh plaice and hake, halibut, lemon sole and mussels. Keep your eye on the specials boards because they sometimes have skate and cod, as well as grilled sardines. The fish is portioned in the shop, a job that used to be done by the chairman of Leeds United Football Club, Peter Ridsdale. If you fancy something a bit different, try the potato scallops, dipped in batter and fried.

After smashing the Aussies all over Headingly Cricket Ground in 1981, Ian Botham went to Bryan's to celebrate.

Bizzie Lizzies

36 Swadford Street, Skipton, Yorkshire
Mon–Thurs 11.30am–11.15pm, Fri–Sat 11.30am–midnight, Sun midday–11.15pm • Busiest weekends

Skipton is another example of a pretty Yorkshire market town and attracts tourists to its Norman-based castle, canal trips and lively centre. Consequently, the streets can be a bit of a crush in the summer. People come from all corners of the galaxy to visit this world-famous shop and few are ever disappointed.

Bizzie Lizzies is perched on a rise overlooking the canal and

the higgledy-piggledy charm of the houses lining it, and is run by Jean and her two sons, Alan and Mark Ritson. Jean has been buying and frying for over 25 years and took over the business here 15 years ago. It benefits from a

Patrick Stewart (Captain Jean-Luc Picard of the *Starship Enterprise*), is one customer who beams down regularly to

48

spacious takeaway area with at least five tills going most of the time, plenty of efficient and friendly staff, a bad-weather eating area and a cool and comfortable restaurant with great views. Jean has taken inspiration from American fast-food outlets yet has made sure her shop has lost none of the charm of a traditional independent chippy.

The most popular fish here is cod from Iceland, but haddock is also available together with a much greater range of fish in the restaurant. The batter is of their own devising, producing a light, crunchy golden finish, sealing the fish beautifully. They blanch their thick chips before flash-frying them to create an impressively crisp outer coating. If you can't resist eating outside, the food is wrapped in paper only and you can sit on the towpath, watching the boats pass by.

Bizzie Lizzies. This shop is considered to have boldly gone where no one has gone before.

Millers Cafe and Takeaway

55 The Village, Haxby, York, Yorkshire

Mon 5–10.30pm, Tues–Sat 11.30am–1.30pm/evening hours vary • Busiest on Friday and Saturday

The community of Haxby lies on the outskirts of York. Set back from the main road, Millers Cafe and Takeaway consists of a large counter and a small, partially concealed area at the side containing a few tables. The shop is now run by half-brothers Steve and David Miller, who took it over from David's father.

The cod is bought fresh from the Faroe Isles and the haddock from Scotland, both occasionally supplemented by fish from

Norway or Iceland. Although they like to use thickly cut Maris Pipers for the chips here, they also have a penchant for French potatoes. The mushy peas are freshly made and have a zingy taste.

Sean Connery was the outright winner of a survey to find out who we'd secretly love to serve us our fish and chips.

Frying Squad

110 Lytham Road, Blackpool, Lancashire
Summer (mid-July to mid-Sept), daily 11.30am–midnight; winter, Fri–Sun 11.30am–midnight

Frying Squad provides good quality and well-prepared fish, plus a winter service of sorts (albeit somewhat skeletal) for the people who don't disappear when the sun does. Frank and Kevin Coward have owned this shop for six years and bring in their fish, all of it fresh, from Scotland via Fleetwood. They portion it in the shop and serve it – mostly cod, haddock and plaice – with the skin off, boned and dipped in a standard batter that they have

enlivened in some secret way. Their goal is an ultra-crisp and wafer-thin batter. They cut medium-sized chips, which is unusual for an area where thick ones are the norm, and make their own mushy peas.

He was chosen by 26 per cent of women respondents. Catherine Zeta Jones came out on top for the men.

St Anne's

41 St Andrew's Road, Lytham St Anne's, Lancashire
Mon–Sat 11.45am–1.30pm/5–9pm • Busiest on Friday

Lytham St Anne's is the central meeting place of Lytham and St Anne's, two small settlements that have spread along the duney coast so that, were it not for the road signs, you wouldn't realize they were once separate. The place is known as the slightly upmarket version of Blackpool (which is just down the coast) and for having an international-standard golf course, which

sometimes hosts the British Open. The town's architecture mainly consists of handsome Georgian, Victorian and Edwardian buildings and the post-war villas that have evolved into guesthouses and hotels.

The custom is regular and local, boosted by tourists in the summer, but Stephen says, "You can't have a goo

The St Anne's chippy hides its comfortable and intimate restaurant behind the compact facade of the shop, rather like Dr Who's Tardis. Stephen Bellamy has owned the place for ten years, after buying and frying for 20 years before that. He likes to get his fish (which is all fresh) from Scotland via Fleetwood and cuts it up on the premises into hearty portions. As well as haddock and cod they serve hake, halibut and plaice, all boneless. The fish is dipped in batter that is made to order by an excellent company in Blackburn, ensuring that it is light, dry and crispy. They make their own mushy peas and sell a vegetable-based curry sauce, along with the usual accompaniments. Once charged with your goodies, you'll find the seafront is only a five-minute walk away.

eputation without good food, good staff and smart surroundings; you haven't got a good reputation you haven't got a business".

Happy Haddock

156 Watling Street Road, Fulwood, Preston, Lancashire
Mon–Fri 11.30am–2pm, Sat 4.30–9pm

333 Plungington Road, Fulwood, Preston, Lancashire
Mon–Sat 11.30am–2pm/4.30pm–midnight • Busiest all day Friday

Watling Street Road

In some ways Preston is a typical post-industrial town, which apparently has bags of charm (by which tourism officers mean terraced housing, cobbled alleys and large chimneys that no longer smoke) and a jazzed-up high street. It acts as a centre for many of the region's transport systems but in general still retains an air of neglect like a forgotten houseplant.

Within Preston's boundaries are two fish and chip shops that personify two schools of thought – the modern and the traditional. Both are called Happy Haddock and both are operated by Mr P. Mullen, who has worked in the business for 16 years. The first is a modern fan-cooled restaurant and takeaway on a main road in a residential area of detached

Whatever the differences in location between these two shop both are friendly, efficient and well organized, and the mos

Watling Street Road

and semi-detached houses; the second is a typical corner chippy, set among terraced houses. They both serve excellent fish and chips. The fish comes from Iceland or Norway, via Hull, and is boned and portioned in the shops. Originally the main fish of choice was haddock but these days it's cod (though several other options include plaice and rock/huss). The fish is coated in a family batter recipe from at least two generations ago, cooked at about 180°C and served with thickly cut chips. You may also be tempted by the fine home-made fish cakes. This being Lancashire, they soak their mushy peas overnight and take great pride in their flavour and colour, and you'll also find that everyone wants to eat fish on Friday.

Plungington Road

equent phrase you'll hear in either is "Do you want salt and negar with that?".

Fisher's Plaice

29 Westcliffe Drive, Layton, Blackpool, Lancashire
Mon–Sat 11.30am–1.30pm/4.30pm–midnight; winter, closes10.30pm (Sat 9.30pm) • Busiest 4.30–6.30pm

David Taylor bought this little award-winning shop in 2001 and continues the impressive tradition set by Les Evans, his predecessor. The fish is all fresh, brought from Scotland via Fleetwood, and cut up on the premises. The most popular fish in this part of the world is haddock, but the wider selection available offers cod, plaice and rock. Each fish is coated in a made-to-order batter

that seals, crisps and colours well. They like to cut their chips very thickly here, a solid 17mm hunk that complements the fish and goes extremely well with the home-made mushy peas.

A clear advantage of this shop is that, with the exception of hectically busy times, they cook the fish to order.

Kelbrook Fisheries

401 Colne Road, Kelbrook, Lancashire
Mon, Wed, Sun 4–8pm, Thurs/Fri lunchtimes and evenings, Sat 11.45am–10pm • Busiest Fri/Sun

V Ⓢ   Ⓨ Ⓘ◐Ⓘ

Just south of the Yorkshire Dales sits the tiny village of Kelbrook, roughly equidistant from Colne to the south and Skipton to the northeast. It's worth knowing that there has been a fish and chip shop in the village since 1896 and it has had only five careful owners.

On a menu that celebrates the diversity of fish appear the old favourites – cod, plaice and haddock (the haddock special is a

massive 16–32oz) – alongside more unusual entries such as lemon sole, Alaskan pollock, butterfly prawns and salmon fillets. The staples all come from Iceland and are portioned in-house, to a hearty standard size of 8oz.

...mon and Elise always have time for people, which no doubt ...plains why Bobby Robson pays them the occasional visit.

Mere Park Fisheries

252 Preston Old Road, Blackpool, Lancashire
Mon–Sat 11.30am–1.30pm/evenings from 4.30pm • Busiest Thursday, Friday and Saturday

Doreen Edmonds and her son Paul operate this family business as a traditional community fish and chip shop. They are set too far back in the suburban sprawl to worry about tourists in kiss-me-quick hats and they give a year-round service to the people who live nearby, and the regulars who travel miles (from Preston and beyond) to taste their fare. The family has been in the

business for 25 years and on this site for 12. The staple is haddock, followed by cod and plaice. The chips are thick and the home-made mushy peas have won an award. In fact, the shop has won several local awards.

Luminaries like Victor Spinetti (who starred in the Beatle films) have been known to brave the backroads to get her

Seniors

106 Normoss Road, Blackpool, Lancashire

Mon–Sat 11.30am–2pm/4.30–7pm (Thurs–Sat to 8pm during illuminations) • Busiest weekend eves

V **🏠** **🍽**

Although it's right on the outskirts of the town on the way to Fleetwood, this is my favourite Blackpool shop. Seniors has been a small community fish and chip shop for years, serving a residential area and the pub directly opposite. The shop is cosy and brightly decorated, as is the attached restaurant (which has recently been extended and revamped to make it even better), and the

staff are both knowledgeable and efficient. In the shop you can choose from cod, haddock, plaice, halibut, hake, whiting, John Dory, skate and salmon. There are also some spectacularly good fish cakes on offer.

ne local is working his way through the menu; others come
om as far afield as Liverpool once a week to eat the fish.

Cemetery Chippy

75 Keighley Road, Colne, Lancashire

Mon–Sat 11.15am–1.30pm/evenings from 4.15pm• Busiest Friday lunchtime and teatime

The town of Colne could almost be an advert for sliced brown bread, being full of soot-blackened little stone houses and dry-stone walls, narrow streets and steep hills. Hidden in one of these typical Lancashire terraces directly opposite the cemetery is a small and narrow chip shop. This simple traditional shop (though not so traditional as to miss out on having its own website at cemeterychippy.com) is run by Les and Val Scott, who stress the need for quality fish and a good service. They also sponsor local sports teams like Trawden Celtic Junior Football, the

Mini Colts rugby side and Colne Cricket Club juniors, and they also support local school fund-raisers.

With your meal in hand, head over to the graveyard, whic proves a surprising and unexpected pleasure. Hidden behin

The Cemetery Chippy serves mostly cod, although rock, plaice and haddock are also available, which they source from Russia or Iceland via Hull. The fish is all boned and portioned on the premises. Before frying, it's dipped in a standard batter (to which they have added a few secret ingredients) and immersed in piping hot oil. They make a thick-cut chip here and their own tasty, bright green mushy peas. You can take your food over to the pretty graveyard opposite, where Wallace Henry, the bandleader on the *Titanic*, is commemorated – at the path's first crossroads and on the left-hand side you'll find a big white gravestone decorated with a violin. Presumably Henry "played on" as the ship went down.

large Victorian stone archway, it tumbles down one side of a steep alley and overlooks the lush green fields that climb the other side.

The Good Catch

1 Ormskirk Road, Upholland, Skelmersdale, Lancashire
Mon–Sat 11am–2.15pm/4–11pm • Busiest all day on Friday and Saturday

V Ⓩ

Upholland, just outside Skelmersdale, is a pretty unspectacular sort of settlement. It operates more as a commuter zone than anything else, full of old workers' cottages, new executive semis and hundreds of bungalows. This is probably why it contains an excellent little main-road fish shop.

At the back of this chippy is a wet fish shop that, curiously, is owned and run by someone else, but the chip shop is the property of Brian Ashurst, who has owned the place for four years and strives to "produce a quality product consistently". The chief interest here is cod, but small amounts of haddock, plaice and rock/huss are also on the menu. Brian skins and bones the cod and portions it to around 5oz for a standard piece. Along with the medium-cut chips, they also make good well-steeped mushy peas here.

The customer who racks up the most miles is from Canada – he visit once a year and never fails to buy a bag of chips.

New Granada

5 North Albert Street, Fleetwood, Lancashire

Daily 11.30am till evening (closing hours vary). Closed Sundays from September-Easter

Fleetwood combines all the best elements of the rock and floss culture of Blackpool with the quieter and more relaxed feel of Lytham St Anne's. In the centre and near the tramlines is New Granada, the best fish and chip shop in Fleetwood, although Christopher Day has only been running it for a year. In that short time, he has built up a regular customer base of committed locals and visitors.

He buys Icelandic cod, haddock and plaice, which are portioned and boned on the premises, while the chips are thickly cut. For eating out you'll find many benches in the town, situated along the river mouth or the front.

Here they do promotions with the local newspaper such as a "buy one get one free" voucher – worth looking out for.

Hodgson's

96 Prospect Street, Lancaster, Lancashire
Mon–Sat 11.30am–1.30pm/eves from 4.30pm (closing hours vary) • Busiest Friday 4.30–6.30pm

Largely sporting Georgian architecture and sitting by the Lancaster Canal and the River Lune, Lancaster is a pretty if moribund town, compensating for its decline by sandblasting its old buildings to look like new. Lancaster contains many of the attractive features of old Lancashire but few of its harsh and pressing economic problems. Nonetheless, it has had to adjust its sense

of self, since it relies as heavily on the influx of students and tourists as it once did on incoming slaves.

Not far from the town centre, just over the canal, an old terraced housing estate blends seamlessly with the rest of the

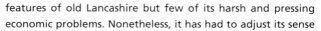

In a relatively short time, Nigel and Linda Hodgson have gained an impressive reputation throughout the county.

town, mostly occupied by long-term elderly residents and students. In one of the terraced houses among these backstreet tenements is the sprightly Hodgson's, run by the unfeasibly young Nigel and Linda Hodgson, who have owned the place for nearly four years. The customer base includes a loyal following from the student population. The fresh fish is delivered each morning from Aberdeen,

and is filleted and portioned on the premises. Their haddock is the most popular choice, although other fish are available. All the fish is dipped in a standard batter that reacts with the vegetable oil heated to 188°C to create a crisp seal and leave the fish steaming gently inside, a perfect accompaniment to the medium-to-thick cut chips. True to Lancashire, they take great pride in their home-made mushy peas.

When you're ready, it's a three-minute walk downhill from the shop to a seat beside the pretty canal just opposite the White Cross pub.

Packet Bridge Fish & Chips

30 Main Road, Bolton-le-Sands, Carnforth, Lancashire
Tues–Sat 11.30am–1pm/evenings from 4.30pm (closing hours vary) • Busiest Friday and Saturday

Bolton-le-Sands is a small, picturesque village just inland from the coast and adjacent to the A6 between Lancaster and Carnforth. It has a canal and towpath, a hump-backed stone bridge, a variety of pubs and an excellent fish and chip shop, which sits between the centre of the village and the main road. If you're driving at any sort of speed you'll miss it, so keep an eye out.

John Wilde has owned the shop since 1999, but it has existed

since 1925. When John started, he knew very little about frying fish, so he embarked on a pretty steep learning curve in a relatively short period of time. I'm pleased to say

The shop's reputation has regularly brought people from all over th place, including well-known customers such as Jim Bowe

66

that he has managed it, though he's modest and open-minded enough to say he still has plenty to learn. His fish is from Norway (principally cod, haddock, plaice and lemon sole), which he portions in the shop and serves with the skin off and boned, together with thickly cut chips. He makes up a variation on a standard batter mix and fries the fish

in vegetable oil at 180–190°C, until the batter shines like a whisky and soda. Alfresco dining can be enjoyed on the towpath five minutes' walk up the road and in a pretty sp⁄ where the trees overhang the canal.

Locals comprise the main custom here, and John knows of them so well that he prepares their order before the⁄ Finally, check out the magnificent Frank Ford clock t of the counter, which is an art deco delight.

Andy's

55 Marlborough Road, Accrington, Lancashire
Mon–Fri 11.30am–1.30pm/evenings from 4.30pm, Sat 4.30–7.30pm • Busiest Wed, Thurs, Fri

The small town of Accrington lies between Burnley and Blackburn. It's a conglomeration of shops, stone terraced houses and retirement bungalows. It smacks of pre- and post-war pragmatism and creates a contrast to the green valley and hills that surround it.

The best chippy in town is owned by Andy Stevensoa, of Cypriot descent, who bought it four years ago, making a radical departure from his old job with the gas board. His shop is an echo of the tiny, old, front-room chippies that used to fill working-class streets with a welcoming smell. From the ground floor of a cramped house in a hunched terrace this chippy provides excellent Icelandic fish. Hake, haddock and plaice are all on sale, but people here want cod more than anything else. The batter produces a crisp outer layer on melt-in-the-mouth fish, and the chips are thickly cut.

The philosophy behind this business is the traditional air for "consistent quality and excellent value for money".

Langley Friery

227 Wood Street, Middleton, Manchester, Lancashire
Mon–Sat 11.30am–11pm, Sunday 4–11pm • Busiest Friday 4–6.30pm

Langley Friery lives by its regular and mostly local custom, so no wonder Sotos Yiasoumis and his staff have an ongoing relationship with their customers. As Yiasoumis says, "Professionalism is the key – don't serve anything that you wouldn't eat yourself, give one hundred per cent, choose quality ingredients and make friends with both the customers and the staff".

The demand here is for fresh cod only, which comes from Peterhead or Aberdeen. This is portioned into standard-sized pieces of about 5oz (larger sizes are also available), immersed in batter and plunged into oil for a golden, crisp finish. When you break open the batter a satisfying column of steam rises from the bright white fish. The chips are cut in the shop to medium thickness and served, according to local tastes, with home-made mushy peas that have been soaked overnight.

his straightforward little shop has recently been voted ish and Chip Shop of the Neighbourhood".

Jackson's Supper Bar

24a Church Street, Wilmslow, Cheshire
Mon–Fri 11.15am–2pm/5pm–midnight, Sat 11.15am–midnight, Sun 5pm–midnight • Busiest weekends

Roger Jackson has worked in the fish-frying business for 30 years and in this excellent little takeaway for 25 of them. He serves large portions, predominantly cod and haddock, but also plaice, skate or rock, all from the North Atlantic via Smithfield Market. The fish is skinned, cut into 7–8oz pieces and boned on the premises, while the batter has been adapted from a standard mix which, together with the very high temperature of the oil (a clever combination of groundnut and vegetable oil), seals the fish beautifully and cuts down on the grease. Unusually for a chippy, Roger prefers to use King Edwards to make his chips, though he will use Maris Piper potatoes when the Kings are not available, but it makes little difference as his chips are a thick-cut perfection. For extras why not try the home-made mushy peas, winner of the Batchelor's Mushy Pea Award?

One famous customer to grab a takeaway from this excellent chippy is **Shirley Bassey**, who ate it sitting in a Rolls-Royce

Les's

51 Victoria Street, Crewe, Cheshire
Mon—Wed 11am–4.30pm, Thurs–Fri 11am–6pm, Sat 11am–4.30pm • Busiest Thurs–Sat

 🍽

This large, bright, spotlessly clean business is owned by Les and Michele Manning. In the restaurant, they offer a range of traditional meals, like the fish dinner for a fiver (consisting of fish, chips and peas, bread and butter, and a pot of tea or coffee).

It's a family-run affair with long-standing and loyal staff, who obviously feel like part of the family, too. The main focus is on

cod, but you can also buy plaice, haddock, skate and rock, plus a variety of other fish in the restaurant. The chips are crisp and tasty, and they make their own mushy peas, as well as a vegetable-based curry sauce and gravy.

This chippy was awarded "fish and chip shop of the year" for the millennium (2000), as judged by the Sea Fish Industry Authority.

Admirals

10 The Square, Hale Road, Halebarns, Cheshire
Mon–Fri 11.30am–2pm/4.15–9pm, Sat 4.15–9pm • Busiest 4.15–6.30pm and bank holidays

Situated in another so-called village just outside Manchester, but in truth more a posh suburb of the city, is this excellent little takeaway hidden at the back of one of those late sixties/early seventies shopping squares. Edward Case has been buying and frying fish for 34 years, the last seven of which he has spent at this location, and as chip-shop owners go he is something of a philosopher, choosing to paraphrase a line from the Kevin Costner movie,

Field of Dreams, "If you build it they will come". Ed's version is "If it's any good they will come". He has a point, since his shop draws custom from both the locals and the surrounding districts.

One celebrity customer at Admirals was Rod Stewart who, whe
playing in Manchester, ordered food on two consecutive night

Over and above that, his customers come to sample the cod, haddock, plaice and salmon or home-made luxury fish cakes. Most of the raw fish comes from Aberdeen, Peterhead or the Shetlands and, according to Ed, has a sweeter taste than fish from elsewhere. The fish is skinned, boned and generously portioned on the premises before being cooked in a standard batter mix – "you get a good batter through elbow grease, not trickery". Nothing but the finest palm oil is used for frying the fish, and it's kept good and hot and replaced entirely each week for freshness.

As for the accompanying chips, they are thickly cut and go well with a dollop of Admirals' soaked-overnight mushy peas, curry sauce made with beef suet, their own madras sauce or the home-made gravy which is also on offer. The best place to eat your meal is in the square, with its benches and somewhat undernourished trees.

Another customer – celebrating his birthday – decided to have several portions wrapped in the *Financial Times*.

The Poynton Fish Bar & The Ladybrook

The Poynton Fish Bar, 49 London Road South, Poynton, Cheshire
The Ladybrook, 12 Fir Road, Bramhall, Cheshire
Both shops, Mon–Fri 11.30am–1.30pm/4.30–10pm, Sat 11.30am–2pm/4.30–9pm

Brian Lowery owns two chippies in this region, both run in much the same fashion. They may be nothing special to look at, but as purveyors of good fish and chips they deserve your consideration. The Poynton shop lies just off a main road and has a dedicated parking area in front of it; The Ladybrook is a typical

The Poynton Fish Bar

inclusion in the shopping area of a housing estate. Brian has owned the Poynton shop for two years and the Bramhall one for three, making the best use of his 30 years' experience in

Both shops have an impressively loyal following considering the relatively short time that they have had to

74

buying and frying to provide a consistent product and service.

The benefit of long-standing connections in the fish-supply trade means that both of the shops receive fresh cod

The Ladybrook

from Grimsby, and plaice and haddock from the Manchester Fish Market. All the fish is portioned in-house to make pieces big enough for a hungry man and prepared for frying without the skin or bones. It is dipped in a well-beaten standard batter that emerges from pure vegetable oil heated to 145–150°C as an ultra thin dry coating that breaks crisply over the juicy blue-white fish. Cooked in the same oil are thickly cut chips that can be accompanied by some smooth home-made mushy peas and a choice of sauces, including a home-made madras curry sauce that lifts toupees and leaves nuns red in the face.

Despite their reputations and long-distance regulars, both are predominantly community shops involved in local charities, helping with school fund-raising and providing good cheap grub to the local residents.

stablish themselves and, gratifyingly, their reputations have pread far enough to encourage customers from many miles away.

Dolphin Fish & Chips

30–34 Scarisbrick Avenue, Southport, Merseyside
Feb–Oct, every day 11am–7pm; Nov–Jan hours vary • Busiest weekends and school holidays

 except haddock

In between the imposing Georgian and Victorian edifices of Southport's main road (which were built to distract you from the fact that the town's financial origins were in the less-than-respectable trade of the Liverpool docks), a few narrow pedestrian alleys lead to the promenade. In the middle of one such walkway is Dolphin, a famous fish and chip shop and the public face of a

fish-frying dynasty stretching back to the Second World War. In fact this is one of England's oldest family frying endeavours. In 1982, the shop was passed down from father to son to the current caretakers, Mr and Mrs

Dolphin operates constantly for nine months of the year but, like Southport, goes quiet for the rest of the year. When it's open, it's

Handley, who will no doubt pass the business on to their own children when the time comes. Indeed Dolphin has a decidedly

traditional feel, concentrating as it does on cod, haddock and plaice, all from Scotland via Fleetwood. The Handleys serve all the fish (except the haddock) with the skin off and boned, and use a fine biscuit mix to create their own batter, which produces a crisp finish. They cut a thick chip here, fry everything in pure vegetable oil at about 165–175°C and make their own mushy peas. Check out the blackboards, which advertise special deals in the restaurant and variations on the types of fish available. If you decide to eat alfresco you have the choice of either heading for the sea, via the Marine Lake (two minutes' walk), or opting for Lord Street's imposing architecture (one minute's walk) and the benches near the bandstand surrounded by flowerbeds, where you can relax and watch the world go by.

ousy with locals and visitors, mainly due to its reputation for putting "good quality food in front of the customers".

Mr Chips

5 Preston New Road, Churchtown, Southport, Merseyside
Mon–Sat and bank holidays 11.30am–1.45pm/5–10.30pm • Busiest Friday

Southport is a grand seaside resort just up the coast from Liverpool to which well-to-do Scousers used to retire. Mr Chips is found on a main road and is surrounded by housing and local shops. It qualifies as a traditional community shop, since it sponsors various local charities and sports teams, but the owner has tried to introduce new ideas and methods. It's been owned for the last seven years by Stephen Stannard, who firmly believes in taking pride in "cleanliness, efficient service and a good basic product". The biggest demand is for cod, so he sticks almost exclusively to that, sourcing it from Scotland via Fleetwood. Stephen cuts medium chips, produces some excellent home-made mushy peas and provides free tomato sauce. The food is wrapped so well that it will still be warm after the 15-minute drive to the seafront.

If you have a complaint about your fish you'll get a refund and a free meal. I'll bet they don't have to do that very often.

Plumtrees

99 Nottingham Road, Keyworth, near Nottingham, Nottinghamshire
Mon–Sat midday–1.45pm/5–10pm • Busiest 5–8.30pm daily

V **S**

Central Nottingham is only 10 minutes from Plumtrees, a local community chip shop that nestles in a small village. The family of the owner, Peter Piponides, got him into the fish and chip trade at an early age and since then he has been buying and frying for 20 years, the last five in this shop. He follows the tradition of local fish shops that look after their customers and provide a worthwhile product, which is also good value for money – in other words, "restaurant food at takeaway prices". Each day the shop receives a fresh fish delivery from Grimsby, most of which is haddock portioned in-house into large 8–10oz pieces. Other fish include cod, tuna, plaice, skate, swordfish, salmon and shark. The end result is a delicious and extremely healthy combination, testament to Peter's crusade to produce the healthiest fish and chips around.

Peter says, "We try to be innovative, have a strong tradition, and look for ways to improve what we do for the customer".

St James's Fish Restaurant

Brighowgate, Great Grimsby, South Humberside
Mon–Thurs 11.30am–8pm, Fri–Sat 11.30am–9pm • Busiest market days and weekends

V **S**

Behind the simple frontage of this typical community fish and chip shop beats a heart of pure golden crispiness. The paramount fish here is the chunky and flavoursome haddock (caught locally or imported but always fresh). The restaurant also specializes in filleted halibut and skate wings.

The big decision, if you're not eating in the decent-sized traditional restaurant, is where to indulge yourself. Some locals plonk themselves down on the step outside the shop and tuck in, but visitors might want to walk the 20 or so metres across to St James's Square in the shadow of the church. There you can people-watch from one of the benches, although you may have to beat off the urchin-sized pigeons. Just across from the square is the Covered Market, which is open every Tuesday, Wednesday, Friday and Saturday.

This hybrid of character and excellent value is owned by a fish merchant, and he's not shy about giving you plenty to eat.

Elite Fish and Chip Shop/Restaurant

Moorland Shopping and Industrial Complex/Centre, Tritton Road, Lincoln, Lincolnshire
Mon 11.30am–7.30pm, Tues–Sat 11.30am–9.30pm, Sun 11.30am–7.30pm • Busiest weekends

B ✂ except plaice and skate   ☖ ⦿

This modern take on a traditional shop attracts three core types of customer: office workers, retired folk and families.

The shop consists of a walk-through takeaway and a large restaurant. Whatever your taste you'll be guaranteed excellent haddock, cod, plaice, rock salmon/huss or skate (all bought in Hull) and thickly cut chips. The fish is skinned and boned – except the plaice and skate – and dipped in a batter made to a long-cherished, secret family recipe.

The choice of extras is typical of this part of the world (gravy, curry sauce and mushy peas), with the bonus of baked beans. If eating in the restaurant, you can enjoy a tipple from the bar. This is the sort of place that attracts no-nonsense fish and chip lovers, which probably explains why Jim Bowen (one-time *Bullseye* presenter) agreed to open it.

This shop scooped "Chippy O' T' Year" in 1996 and the Fish and Chip shop of the Year award in 1992, from the Sea Fish Industry Authority.

Ernie Beckett's

21 Market Street, Market Place Corner, Cleethorpes, near Grimsby, Lincolnshire
Mon–Sat 11.30am–9pm, Sun 11.30am–6pm • Busiest in summer, and weekend evenings

B **S**

This smart-looking fish and chip shop is situated on the main drag just 50 metres from the beach. Ernie ran the shop until he died but Reg Smith now owns the place and kept the name as a mark of respect.

This is a big haddock area, but you can also try the plaice or the skate. All the fish is coated in a crunchy golden batter, and they make their own mushy peas, gravy and curry sauce. The food is expertly wrapped – in fact, Reg

has demonstrated his talent on *The Generation Game*. If you don't want to eat in the restaurant, seafront benches are a dawdle away. You might even spy John Prescott indulge in a large haddock and chips.

Grimsby Evening Telegraph held a competition in the 1990s to find the best fish and chip shop in the area: this shop came out on top.

St Anne's

9–11 Victoria Rd, Mablethorpe, Lincolnshire
Summer, Mon–Sun 11am–11pm; winter, Mon–Sun 11am–2pm/5–11.30pm • Busiest in summer

Dotted sporadically along the Lincolnshire coast between Skegness and Cleethorpes are a number of small resort towns. Mablethorpe is one such town and its best fish and chip shop is set one street back from the beachfront. It's a labour of love for David Muggeson, who bought the shop to fulfil an ambition that he cherished during those cold lonely mornings on his milk round. The menu in St Anne's offers cod, haddock, skate, plaice and rock salmon. The cod and haddock come fresh from Grimsby and are caught by long-line fishing, in a bid to preserve stocks by avoiding the netting of juveniles and small egg-carrying fish. The skate, plaice and rock come via the fish markets. The fish and the thickly cut chips (since we're in Lincolnshire they get the pick of the Maris Pipers) are all fried at 180–190°C, an takeaway food is wrapped in paper only.

hose wishing to can make the most of the unprete
00-seater restaurant where you can BYO (Bring Your Own

Silver Fish

3 North Street East, Uppingham, Rutland
Mon–Sat 11.30am–2pm/4.30–10.30pm • Busiest on Friday

V **S**

Uppingham is a pretty village, not far from
the water sports and bird-spotting delights
of Rutland Water. The reason this village has
survived so well is that it is the home of
Uppingham Public School.

This may not be the sort of place you would
expect to find a great chippy, but nonetheless, just as Rowan
Atkinson (an ex-Uppingham boy) confounded his masters, it
does indeed have one. The Silver Fish has been owned and run
for two years by Varnavass Georgiou who produces some
excellent fare for locals, schoolboys and their visiting parents,
ers-by and others on their way to Rutland Water.

all comes from Grimsby – cod, haddock or plaice – and
n it on the premises. You might expect a refined
p, but they dish out pretty thick "soldiers" that
a spoonful of the home-made mushy peas.

tious,
wine.

allies (pickled gherkins) try out their tasty
pickled gherkins.

Brownsover Fish Bar

124–126 Hollowell Way, Rugby, Warwickshire
Mon–Sat 11.30am–2pm/eves from 4.30pm • Busiest Thursday, Friday, and Saturday 4.30–6.30pm

V **S** haddock and plaice **S** cod

Rugby is a typical Midlands town, between
Coventry and Northampton, famous for the
invention of rugby football at Rugby School.
Standing proud in one of several suburbs is
the Brownsover Fish Bar. Owned and run by
Andrew and Yasmine Thrasyuoulou (and their
loyal manager, Hazel), the shop has been in the family for at
least 20 years. Andy's parents retired in 1992 and since then he
and Yasmine have doubled its size. The choice of fish consists
of haddock, cod and plaice – all delivered fresh daily from
Grimsby, boned and portioned in-house into generous 8oz
slices. To prepare it for the pan, the fish is dipped in a standard
batter that gives a light golden colour and a thin crisp coating
after frying in vegetable oil at 140–170°C. The home-made
accompaniments include a vegetable-based curry sauce,
smooth mushy peas and a pungent meat-based gravy.

ghty per cent of Brownsover's custom is local, but regulars
so come from as far away as Wales, drawn by its reputation.

Hillmorton Fish Saloon

68 Featherbed Lane, Hillmorton, near Rugby, Warwickshire
Mon–Sat 11.45am–2pm/evenings from 5pm • Busiest Friday 5–6.30pm and Saturday lunchtimes

 haddock cod

Situated on a big residential estate, on the opposite side of Rugby from the Brownsover Fish Bar (p85), is the Hillmorton Fish Saloon. This neat and well-kept chip shop is owned by Nick Phedon and his father. The father has owned the business since 1977 but, these days, he tries to take a back seat. Most people in the area prefer cod and haddock, both of which are delivered fresh – the cod from Grimsby and the haddock from Aberdeen. The fish is portioned on the premises and dipped in a slightly modified batter mix. The chips are cut to a middle thickness and can be accompanied by home-made mushy peas. Once your meal is ready, they offer a choice of paper or cardboard-box wrapping. About 70 per cent of the people who walk through the door are locals, and the rest are a combination of passing trade and regulars who come from miles away.

Nicholas Parsons says, "The British have turned a simple nourishing dish into a national institution. Fish and chip

Heathcote Fish Bar

86 Heathcote Road, Whitnash, Leamington Spa, Warwickshire
Mon–Sat midday–2pm & 4.45–10pm • Busiest Friday 4.45–6.30pm and evening

 cod

David Hine has worked in the fish-frying industry for 13 years, training from the age of 19, and in this location for six years.

The most popular fish consumed at the Heathcote Fish Bar are cod, haddock and plaice, all delivered fresh daily from Aberdeen and portioned in-house. David uses a standard batter to coat his fish, which is fried at 170–190°C, while he cuts thick chips and soaks his home-made mushy peas overnight. The food is

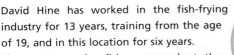

dished up in paper bags, then wrapped in more paper. If you eat in your car opposite the shop, you can appreciate the calm and efficient air of the staff.

e now as synonymous with our country as Shakespeare,
icket and the Tower of London ...".

Although fish and chips are still hugely popular today, it is interesting how many people have a sense of nostalgia for the nation's favourite takeaway.

Top model Jodie Kidd says, "I've loved fish and chips since I was a little girl; they form an important part of many people's childhood and daily lives."

The
South

Rafferty's

67 Occupation Road, Corby, Northamptonshire
Daily evenings, Tues–Sat lunchtimes also (hours vary) • Busiest Friday and Saturday

V **S**

About halfway between Northampton and Peterborough is Corby, one of the new towns of the 1950s and 60s. You'll find Rafferty's about three minutes' drive from the centre of Corby.

Set in a red-brick housing estate, along with a pub and off-licence, the shop stands out with its striking black-and-pink signage. Here you'll find cod, haddock and

plaice, as well as cockles and mussels, which are delivered fresh from Grimsby. It is worth remembering that there is a 200-acre wooded park in the middle of the town.

A sign requests that you order your meal before joinir the queue, so that you don't have to hang about.

90

The Sandringham

25–27 Tower Street, King's Lynn, Norfolk

Mon–Fri 10.30am–6pm, Sat 10am–6pm • Busiest on market days (Tues and Sat) and lunchtimes

V **S** unless otherwise requested

The historic market town of King's Lynn is more of a shellfish than cod area, so there are only a few fish shops here. However, the one that stands out is good-value, no-nonsense and well worth a visit.

The shop is a family-run business of ten years' standing, and sells mostly cod to locals and visitors, although they also offer haddock and plaice from the Norwegian fleet. They pride themselves on the generosity of their portions and serve the fish boned and with the skin on (unless you ask them to do otherwise) in a crisp batter, fried with large, golden chips. If you ask for an open bag of fish and chips you'll get your choice of curry sauce or gravy free of charge. For pensioners the shop does a specially priced fish and chip meal. Finally, the shop is a mere five-minute stroll from the riverside, where you can sit and watch the ducks quack about.

It's no surprise that Brian McNeirney, history professor and Anglia Television personality, included this shop in his *Rivers* series.

Quayside Chippy

The Quay, Wells-next-the-Sea, Norfolk
Summer, daily 11.45am–10pm; winter, Mon–Sat 11.45am–7pm • Busiest in summer and on Fridays

It's hard to imagine a more atmospheric and, in many ways, attractive place to have a fish and chip shop than opposite the quay in the tiny community of Wells-next-the-Sea. From the shop you can walk across the road and look out over the estuary and its picture-postcard little harbour, or up the long flat coast almost as far as Blakeney Point – a natural spit owned by the National Trust

and hosting rare birds and a seal colony. Many of the buildings still retain the ancient block-and-tackle beams jutting out from their upper storeys, where cargo would have been hauled up for storage or

Despite some bad press, fish and chips make a high nutritious meal and, with thick-cut chips, are relatively lo

lowered for passage on the trading boats.

The Quayside Chippy, with its tiny eating area, sits next door to a small amusement arcade and a few tourist shops, and similar arcades cover a good proportion of what would once have been a busy dockside. The chip shop has made a refreshing step backwards, having been converted from an American diner to a purveyor of traditional English fare. It is owned by the Grey family, who have been in the seaside entertainment and food industries for about 40 years.

The fish on offer is a traditional menu of cod, haddock, plaice, or rock/huss, all of which comes from Norway and is portioned on the premises. It is served with the skin on, boned and dipped in a straightforward batter mix that reacts with the oil to form a golden colour and a smooth crunchy texture. Both the fish and the medium-to-thick chips are fried in beef dripping (quite unusual for the area) at 175–180°C and served with the usual extras, including some good pickles.

fat. Model and TV presenter Melinda Messenger swears by them:
love fish and chips", she says, "I eat them at least twice a week".

93

Park Chippy

37 Station Road, Suffield Park, Cromer, Norfolk
Tues–Sat lunchtimes and evenings (hours vary – open later July and Aug) • Busiest Friday/Saturday

The second excellent fish and chip shop in the pocket-sized Cromer (see Mary Jane's, p96) – a town at the mercy of the bracing North Sea winds – is about four minutes' drive from the town centre and the seashore. Although its location is not exactly "in your face", the Park Chippy still does a roaring trade, which speaks volumes for its reputation, both in the town and throughout the region.  The shop is run by David Audley and his family. David has worked in the buying and frying trade for a little over 15 years and on this site for over five.

As a direct result of a free write-up in *The Observer* a wh
ago, the Park Chippy draws regular customers from as f

94

Because the shop is situated slightly inland, it has the feel of a community business rather than a tourist chippy. As a result, well over half of the regular customers are locals, and about 20 per cent drive into town from the surrounding area on a regular basis; the rest of the custom is made up of passing tourists and part-time locals staying at the nearby caravan parks.

The shop offers a wide variety of fish, but mainly deals in cod from the Faroe Isles, which is portioned on the premises. Before it is fried in beef dripping at 170–178°C, the fish is dipped in a standard batter mix that has been slightly tweaked by David to make a thin yet firm coating with a clean taste.

Since Cromer is not a million miles from the Fens, the shop uses Fenland Maris Piper potatoes for its chips. These potatoes have their own subtly distinctive flavour and are cut to a medium thickness, before being fried at 175–180°C.

As far as extras are concerned, the Park Chippy is one of the few fish and chip shops to specialize in mint mushy peas, which are a refreshing complement to the chips. In the summer months, they also make an onion gravy, especially for the northerners who descend on the town like the Viking hordes of yore.

vay as Wales and Scotland, which proves that people will go any stance for a decent piece of fish and a good bag of chips.

Mary Jane's

27–29 Garden Street, at the corner of Garden and Corner streets, Cromer, Norfolk

Daily 11.30am–11pm (closed Christmas Day) • Busiest at weekends and in summer

B **S** unless otherwise requested

Hunched on cliffs above its lifeboat station, Cromer turns its back on North Sea winds in the winter yet celebrates its proximity to the beach in the summer. In the old town the streets are tight and narrow, and Mary Jane's stands out like a beacon. It's a family business,

which was passed down to the current keeper, Grant Zelos, by his father. The fish is the best quality and is dipped in a smooth

batter. The chips are thick-cut, while the mushy peas are soaked overnight and cooked freshly each day. Finding a place to eat is not difficult, since it's only a minute's walk to the cliffs where you can sit and watch the seabirds.

Mary Jane's has been visited by comedian and actor Mike Rei Rowan Atkinson and most of the Norwich Football Team.

The Bounty

115 High Road West, Felixstowe, Suffolk
Mon–Sat 11.30am–2pm/4.45–10pm • Busiest on Friday

V **S**

It might have struggled as a seaside resort but Felixstowe has turned into a commercial success with its ferry services and the busiest container port in the country. Within one suburb is an excellent chippy, inviting local residents with a warm glow from its open door.

The Bounty, mercifully not run by Captain Bligh, is a traditional corner fish and chip shop within two minutes' drive of the town's stony beaches. The current management have been installed since 1989, serving cod, rock/huss, plaice, skate and haddock, all dipped in a creamy batter. They like to use freshly caught local produce when available, but the supply is so inconsistent that they supplement it with Norwegian fish.

For their medium to thick chips they use a combination of Maris Piper and Blackland potatoes. Those who can't wait to tuck in can make use of the two tables just outside the door.

ne customer from New York liked the food so much he ought several portions, which he transported to America.

Eat Inn

73 High Street, Wickham Market, Suffolk
Mon–Sat 11.30am–1.45pm/4.30–10pm • Busiest Friday and Saturday 4.30–6.30pm

The Eat Inn has been family run since 1967 and is now in the hands of Neill Pearce. Whenever possible, Neill buys fresh fish from Lowestoft or Fleetwood, but he supplements this with fish from Norway and the Faroe Isles. Portioning takes place in the shop to produce a standard piece weighing in at around 6oz and a large piece at 10oz. The menu shows a pretty standard selection, with one or two unusual additions, but most people concentrate on cod, haddock, rock/huss and locally caught skate, when it's in season. If you're feeling adventurous you can opt for gurnard, a somewhat under-used European catch, or hoki, a tasty fish from the coastal waters of New Zealand. If you don't wish to use the cosy restaurant, queue at the separate takeaway entrance and take your meal across the road to the benches by the square.

Unusually for this area, Neill makes his own mushy peas, and stonking hot chilli sauce for anyone brave enough to try it.

Mark's

32 High Street, Southwold, Suffolk

Summer, Mon–Sun (hours vary); winter, Tues–Sat (hours vary) • Busiest Fri and Sat evenings

The seaside resort of Southwold is perched attractively on cliffs above a stone-and-sand beach and is home to a tall white lighthouse and the famous Adnams Brewery.

When Mark's fish and chip shop came onto the market two years ago, two couples decided to join forces to try to keep it local – Gary and Sally Cuthbert and Alan and Jane Palmer. All four agreed that their aim was to "make the sort of food that we'd want to eat ourselves".

Most people here are after cod, plaice, skate or haddock, but it's also worth keeping an eye on the specials blackboards to see if the delicious Southwold rock/huss is available.

The seafront benches, overlooking the famously expensive beach huts and promenade, are no more than five minutes' walk away.

Aldeburgh Fish and Chip Shop & The Golden Galleon

Aldeburgh Fish and Chip Shop, 226 High Street, Aldeburgh, Suffolk
The Golden Galleon, 137 High Street, Aldeburgh, Suffolk
Takeaway: daily 11.45–2pm/5–9pm • Busiest in summer and Friday and Saturday evenings
Restaurant: summer only: Mon, Wed, Fri, Sat lunchtime and evening; Sun midday–7pm

For many years, the shop at 226 High Street has acted as a place of pilgrimage for hungry people from far and wide, and has been owned and run by the same family, the Cooney's, since 1967. In the summer, it is customary to walk from the shop through the higgledy-piggledy alleys to the seafront, a mere 30 metres away, where you can sit and enjoy your meal to the sound of the gentle lap of the tide on the shingle beach. In winter, people are more inclined to drive further up the High Street to an elevated vantage point along the sea wall. Here you can comfortably tuck in to the excellent haddock and cod (from Norway), plaice, rock/huss and skate (caught locally) as waves

One of the most renowned customers at the Aldeburgh Fish and Chip Shop is Penny, a British bulldog, who sidles up to the sho

crash against the shingle and the sea winds buffet your car.

Owing to the growing pressure of demand, The Golden Galleon has opened just down the road from the original shop (limited to plaice, cod and haddock), together with a restaurant above called the Upper Deck.

In both shops the fish is cut into good-sized pieces with the skin left on. Next it is boned and coated in a standard batter mix that has been beaten until it bubbles, producing a crinkly finish when it emerges from frying in (regularly filtered) beef dripping at about 180°C. As a rule, the thickish chips are made from Maris Piper or Maris Bard potatoes and the only extras at the original shop are mushy peas and salt and vinegar, while The Golden Galleon offers a slightly broader range. Takeaway meals are wrapped in paper and bags to ensure the food stays as hot and fresh as possible before you chow down.

window every Friday lunch- and suppertime (thus bypassing the queue that snakes down the road) to collect her battered sausage.

Wrights

3 East Street, Ware, Hertfordshire
Mon 4.30–9pm, Tues–Fri 11.30am–1.45pm/4.30–10pm, Sat 11.30am–9pm • Busiest on Friday

V S

Steve Morris has worked in the industry for 35 years, during which time he's seen almost everything, so he has the relaxed and straightforward air of a man who knows what he's about. The simple takeaway that he runs has won a plethora of hygiene awards.

The haddock, plaice, skate, cod and rock/huss usually come from the Bering Sea or the Norwegian fleet. This is generously portioned in the shop and served with the skin on and boneless. The batter has been refined over the last 35 years and Steve wouldn't tell me how it was made, but it seals the fish well. Everything is fried in vegetable oil, including the "standard-sized" chips (somewhere between thick and medium). Steve believes in getting good quality raw materials and following tried and tested methods to consistently produce the best.

The locals and people from miles around have come to appreciate the professionalism and attention to quality here

Reg's

70 Ravensdale, Great Clacton Village, Essex

Mon–Sat 11am–2.30pm/4.30–9pm (hours vary in school holidays) • Busiest Fridays and Saturdays

V S

BH

Reg's concentrates on looking after its locals and regulars – "They come all year round" – but if you're a visitor this is where you must come for a taste of the sea.

These days it's run by Timothy Skinner whose grandfather started the whole thing off by working in Billingsgate Fish Market. They use a combination of locally caught fresh fish (when available) and good quality produce from Norway and the Faroe Isles, concentrating on cod, haddock, skate, plaice and rock/huss.

When it comes to finding a suitable place to eat your meal, you're no more than a five-minute drive from the sea.

This shop has been in the family for over 20 years, passed down the line like granny's antique silver spoons.

Graham Wright's

24 Osborne Street, Colchester, Essex
Tues–Thurs 11.30am–2.30pm, Fri 11.30am–7.30pm, Sat 11.30am–7pm • Busiest on Saturday

V **S** **$\mathbb{S}$** coley |O|

Regarded as one of the oldest towns in England and a royalist stronghold during the Civil War, Colchester made little of its historic heritage in the 1970s and 80s when it became rather a dour squaddie town. Since then, the town has picked itself up by redeveloping its centre and placing a greater emphasis on its rewarding tourist attractions, such as the castle, the Dutch quarter and the museum.

This fish and chip shop has been in the same family for 51 years and, before it became a chippy in 1920, it was a pub, dating back to the 1700s. It has its own particular history, which I like almost as much as the food. As a young man, Graham Wright worked for the Ford motorcar company and one day was called out to see the proprietor of a fish and chip shop who had a faulty Ford car. Graham fixed the motor and was

As you chat to Graham, you can see him putting in orders because he's seen someone on their way. He says, "Always please the

introduced to the man's daughter, who had just failed her driving test. He offered to teach her to drive and since then has spent 40 years running what used to be his father-in-law's fish and chip shop. Oh – and, yes, his wife (as she became) did pass her test.

All the fish on the menu is fresh, brought from either Lowestoft or Grimsby, and is boned and served with the skin on, except for the coley. Choose between cod, coley, haddock, skate, rock salmon and usk (the local word for rock eel). The fish is portioned by Graham, who cuts big 8oz pieces and makes his batter from plain old flour and water so that it is not too thick and keeps dry on the inside, forming a simple coat around delicious fish. Everything is cooked in vegetable oil, including the medium-to-thick chips (at 150°C for the fish and 170°C for the chips). As a traditional southeast chippy, Graham frowns upon extras, such as gravy and curry sauce, and concentrates on mushy peas and beans instead.

customer, always take a few moments to have a word with people, to remind yourself that they are people". Need I say more?

Mr Chips

31 High Street, Kinver, Nr Stourbridge, Staffordshire
Mon–Thurs lunchtimes and evenings (hours vary); Fri–Sat midday–10.30pm; Sun midday–6pm

V **S** except haddock

Gerald Lloyd ran a transport cafe for 12 years before he decided to exchange it for the rural pleasures of Kinver, an Elizabethan-style ye-olde-pub kind of beauty spot beside a canal on the edge of the Black Country, just a short drive from Birmingham. The pace of life here is probably just as slow as the barely used canal and the ambience is certainly of a simpler and more relaxed time.

The shop has a glass frontage topped by mock-Tudor beams and from the tables at the front you can watch village life pass by. Gerald buys his fish from Wolverhampton Market, filleting it himself and

One regular customer is the Led Zeppelin rock star, Robert Plant, who no doubt believes the same as Gerald

cutting it into generous portions of 8–10oz, on average. He concentrates on cod, haddock, hake, salmon and plaice, and all the fish is served with the skin on (except the haddock) and boned, in a golden crispy thin batter made to his own formula. The fish is fried in pure vegetable oil at 175–180°C, as are the medium-cut chips, while  among the extras are excellent home-made mushy peas, gravy and vegetable-based curry sauce.

Gerald and his wife have focused on building up a regular local trade and their efforts have been rewarded by a mention in the *Good Food Guide* and the winning of several awards. With the help of this publicity and word of mouth, the shop enjoys regular visits from people travelling quite some distance in order to find the kind of quality they want.

when the latter says, "Only the best is good enough for our customers".

The Royal Fish Bar

197 Stourbridge Road, Halesowen, Birmingham, Midlands
Mon–Sat midday–2pm/evenings from 4.30pm, Sun 4.30–10pm • Busiest Friday and Saturday

V **S**

People tend to think of Birmingham as a huge conglomeration of roads and industries but this does a disservice to an interesting and diverse city. In one suburb is the engaging Royal Fish Bar, adhering to the tradition of Cypriot-run fish and chip shops in the Midlands. Nic Nicodemou has owned the shop for 15 years and it has become part of the landscape.

The shop serves delicious fish from Scotland – cod, haddock, plaice, rock and mini-fish bites (mainly for the kids). It's dipped in a smooth batter mix made from a secret family recipe and the chips are cut good and thick.

The Royal Fish Bar is so popular that it was recently awarded the Golden Chip award.

Rainbow Hill Chippy

24 Astwood Road, Rainbow Hill, Worcester, Worcestershire

Mon–Sat midday–2pm/4.30pm–midnight (later Fri & Sat), Sun 5pm–midnight • Busiest Fri & Sat

Five minutes' drive from the centre of Worcester is the Rainbow Hill Chippy. Since 1999, this shop has been owned by Stelios and Michaelina Xiourrouppas, who have been frying fish in England for about 15 years. Stelios cuts his thickish chips from scratch each day. He believes he has found the best size for a chip so that it cooks perfectly in six minutes, along with the fish, which

is left untouched in the pan for the first two minutes to let the batter seal. For added flavour, they offer excellent mushy peas.

This community shop has a three-tiered price structure, with something for everyone.

This is an old-fashioned community shop where the local customers are at the heart of all the decisions made.

Foley's

Stourport Road, Kidderminster, Worcestershire

Mon–Sat 11.30am–10.30pm, Sun 5–10pm, bank holidays 4.30–10.30pm • Busiest Friday & Saturday

V **S** haddock **𝒮** cod **BH**

Kidderminster sits at one end of the famous Severn Valley Railway, one of the longest and loveliest steam railways still in operation. Another thing to cheer you here is the stonkingly good fish and chip shop. Foley's has long been a family business and is now run by Nick Akathiotis. He prefers fish from Scottish waters and concentrates on high-quality cod, haddock and plaice. All the fish is portioned by hand in the shop and dipped in a standard batter that has been supercharged by secret means. Finally, the fish and the thick chips are fried in the same pan, a method that in this part of the world (and for no apparent reason) is called "the Greek method", producing delicious results. Among the tasty side-order dishes on offer are home-made mushy peas. To enjoy your meal, you can try the quiet delights of leafy Brinton Park, just two minutes' drive away.

Foley's inspires deep loyalty among the locals and has such a good reputation that regulars drive for miles to get here.

Catchems End

134 Kidderminster Road, Bewdley, Worcestershire
Mon–Thurs 11.30am–11.30pm, Fri–Sat 11.30am–midnight • Busiest evenings and Friday lunchtime

Catchems End is found on a fairly busy main road just on the outskirts of Bewdley and is easily identified by its tall black and white frontage. This is an established family business, run principally by George Georgoiu, who has been in the business for about 15 years and takes pride in producing great fish and chips as well as kebabs and faggots. The fish on offer is usually cod, haddock or plaice, fresh from Scotland and shipped in to the town on a regular basis. The medium-cut chips have a crunchy coating and a soft, distinctly flavoured centre.

The shop has a loyal local clientele as well as a group of regulars who travel a considerable distance for their food. This explains why you'll probably find a good-humoured queue snaking through the narrow shop enjoying the mouth-watering aromas.

George claims that he runs his business "the way Liverpool play football", and he has established a strong local following.

Napoli Fish Bar

175 Newport Road, New Bradwell, Milton Keynes, Buckinghamshire
Mon–Sat 11.30am–2pm/4.30–9pm • Busiest on Friday and Saturday

V **S**

The village of New Bradwell lies just on the ragged outskirts of Milton Keynes, its superb chippy surrounded by estate housing and located beside a pleasant tree-dotted triangle of grassland separating it from the main road. In the centre of this green are a few benches near an obelisk clocktower.

Luciano Pilla has been operating from the same shop, which is part of a family business, for about 14 years. Continuity and consistency count for a lot to Luciano, and an array of photographs depict the changing faces of the village shopfront since the turn of the century. It's easy to forget that the district surrounding such a new town as Milton Keynes has a longer history. Luciano's father started in the food industry by opening an Italian restaurant, which also served fish and chips, and soon discovered that although the locals loved the

Luciano buys the best fish he can get his hands on and asked me to tell you that if you don't enjoy the

112

fish they weren't quite ready for the delights of Italian food. After that he stuck with the fish and has never looked back.

Every day, the shop receives a delivery of fresh fish from Whitby and, while focusing on cod and haddock, it also sells rock/huss, plaice and skate. The fish is handcut on the premises into generous portions and served with the skin on and boned, having been dipped in a light batter and fried at a high temperature in the best groundnut oil. As for the chips, Luciano takes a middle-of-the-road approach to their size and uses Maris Pipers – or Javelin when the Maris potatoes are out of season. The philosophy is simple: "People remember what it tastes like, not what it costs".

ood, please let him know, but if you do enjoy it, please be sure to tell your friends.

The Frying Machine

Brook Way, Bradley Stoke, Bristol, Avon
Mon–Sat midday–2pm/5–10pm, Sunday 5–8.30pm • Busiest 5–6.30pm and on Fridays

Bristol has always been a culturally progressive city and it keeps on growing. One part of this spread is a development next to the M5 called Bradley Stoke.

On the estate and next to the giant car park of a supermarket you'll find The Frying Machine, a narrow fish and chip shop with a large open kitchen. The walls are decorated with two extensive maps, one of Bristol and the other of the UK, to occupy people in the queue. The fish comes from Iceland, usually cod and haddock, although they also sell excellent plaice. The fish is coated in a standard batter and fried in groundnut oil at very high temperatures to produce a smooth yet crisp finish and succulent white fish; the perfect accompaniment to their thick chips – crisp on the outside and fluffy inside – and home-made marrowfat mushy peas, which are soaked overnight.

The owner, Jack Garrigan, used to work with explosives but nowadays he prefers putting a bomb under your tastebuds.

Sanders

158 Park Lane, Tilehurst, Reading, Berkshire
Mon–Sat 11.30am–1.45pm/evenings from 4.30pm • Busiest Friday 4.30–6.30pm

V **S**

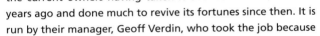

The suburb of Tilehurst lies on Reading's western perimeter, divided by a main road lined with shops. One of these is the neatly decorated red and green Sanders chippy. This friendly shop has existed for many years, the current owners having taken it over seven years ago and done much to revive its fortunes since then. It is run by their manager, Geoff Verdin, who took the job because

of redundancy and has been enjoying the experience ever since. The big sellers here are cod, haddock, rock/huss and plaice, all from the Faroe Isles. The fish is portioned into 6oz standard pieces and served alongside medium-cut chips.

Geoff suggests that you order your fish as soon as you join the queue so that it is cooked while you snake through the shop.

Dorothy's

8 The Square, Harmanswater, Bracknell, Berkshire
Mon–Fri 9.30am–2pm/4.15–9.30pm, Sat 9.30am–9.30pm; open Easter • Busiest Friday evening

V **S** haddock **S** cod

Dorothy's has been owned by the same family since 1985, when they switched from the greengrocery business. The fish is brought from Norway and portioned on the premises "by eye" (hence the decent sizes) and immersed in a standard batter before being fried. The result is a clean batter encasing pure white fish that steams gently inside. The chips, "from the best

potatoes available", are cut to a medium thickness and I recommend the pickles and the home-made mushy peas. If you eat in the restaurant, you'll be well looked after by the experienced and friendly staff.

The shop is well known for producing excellent qualit haddock and, to a smaller demand, rock/huss and plaice.

Cowley Fish Bar

28 High Road, Cowley, Uxbridge, Middlesex
Mon 5–10pm, Tues–Sat midday–2pm/5–10pm • Busiest in the evening and Friday lunchtime

V S

The Cowley Fish Bar has been in the capable hands of Dean Lukic and his wife for the last four years. They seem to understand what makes a successful chip shop: all the staff are family, whether blood relations or not, and the spirit in the shop is second to none.

The catch consists of cod, haddock, rock/huss and plaice – all from the Faroe Isles, Iceland or Russia. This is boned,

and portioned to standard hunks of around 7oz. The preferred thickness of chip here is medium to thick, usually accompanied by either salt and vinegar alone or together with a wallie (pickled cucumber or gherkin).

We aim to provide top quality food, to take great care in the way we cook it, to serve it quickly and to give good value."

Olley's

67–69 Norwood Road, Herne Hill, London SE24
Mon 5–10.30pm, Tues–Thurs midday–3pm/5–10.30pm, Fri/Sat midday–10.30pm, Sun 5–10.30pm

Roughly two minutes' walk from Herne Hill railway station, Olley's produces some of the best fish in south London. The business gets its name from the misspelling of Oliver's, a reference to Charles Dickens's novel *Oliver Twist*, in which fish and chips are mentioned. Take your pick from cod, haddock, plaice, salmon, monkfish, swordfish, halibut, hake, rock/huss and skate – plus whatever

else is available on the day, and a wide selection of grilled fish. For extras try "the best mushy peas in London" (according to *Time Out*), or pea fritters, home-made lemon-and-parsley sauce and all sorts of other options.

People who are passionate about what they do transmit the enthusiasm to everyone else; that's what you'll find at Olley's

Rock and Sole Plaice

47 Endell Street, Covent Garden, London WC2
Mon–Sat 11.30am–11.45pm, Sun 11.30am–10pm • Busiest throughout the summer and weekends

Within two minutes' walk of the tourist cut-and-thrust of Covent Garden is the relative calm of Endell Street, where you will find the third-oldest fish and chip shop in London. It was opened in 1861 and has been dishing up fine fare ever since, earning a mention in over a thousand tour guides of London.

The custom is a cosmopolitan mix, ranging from tourists, local office workers and residents, patrons of the Oasis sports centre opposite in need of a carbohydrate hit, and Londoners from across town. The current owner is Hasan Ziyaeddin, who offers cod, haddock, plaice, Dover sole, rock/huss and skate, all delivered fresh each morning. The chips are particularly thick (and therefore nourishing), owing to a rather unusual cutting blade invented long before the millimetre. If you'd like a bit of colour, try the mushy peas, which are thick and flavoursome.

ere, you may come across such luminaries as Dave Stewart uitarist with the Eurythmics), David Jason and Anthony Hopkins.

119

Geales

2 Farmer Street, Notting Hill Gate, London W8

Mon–Sat midday–3pm/6–11pm, Sun 6–10.30pm • Busiest in summer, and Thurs–Sun evenings

B **V** mixture **S**   🍸 🍽️

Geales of Notting Hill is legendary the world over as one of the best places to eat "good old English fish and chips", a reputation it has held since it opened in 1939 – not even the German bombing of London managed to close its doors. In the past, Geales has had a reputation for being a "posh" fish and chip shop for the well-to-do, but in fact it has always been a "first come, first served establishment", and they make no distinction between the customer who orders cod and chips and a pint of beer, and the one who orders oysters, sea bass and a bottle of champagne. Although Geales is quite clearly a restaurant, it is also a takeaway, despite the absence of a typical takeaway counter. The current owners have run the place for three years (previously the shop had only one owner) and buy their fish fresh every day from Grimsby, the restaurant having kept the

Whichever way you look at it, a visit to Geales is an experience sometimes even a star-studded one (film and pop stars visit in too

120

same fish supplier for 30 years. The range is broad – cod, haddock, rock/huss, plaice, salmon, skate, whitebait, Geales's own delicious fish cakes, and even that old Anglo-Indian favourite, kedgeree. The fish is portioned into large 10oz slices, boned, then dipped in a modified batter recipe, which produces a very light, almost tempura-like finish (in fact they also make a special tempura batter for the Japanese who flock here). The chips are medium to thick with a good texture and, if you like mushy peas, you'll be glad to know that they soak and boil up marrowfat peas to make their own – which they humorously call the English equivalent of Mexican refried beans. They also make their own version of tartare sauce.

reat a proliferation for me to name them individually), and you're uaranteed a good welcome and fantastic fish and chips.

Pap's

23 The Broadway, Southgate, London N14

Mon–Sat 11.30am–3pm/5–11pm • Busiest at lunchtime and on Thursday, Friday and Saturday

V S   Ⓨ 🍽

Modestos Papageorgiou has worked in the trade for over 30 years, and for the last five he has owned and run this intimate, air-conditioned, 54-seater restaurant and shop just two minutes' walk from Southgate Circle. The fish is delivered from Billingsgate and Grimsby markets, and cut into portions of 8–10oz. The menu gives you a choice of cod, haddock, plaice, trout, sea bass,

halibut, sole and salmon, all fried in pure groundnut oil. If you wish, you can have your fish grilled rather than fried. To accompany the meal are medium-to-thick chips and all the usual extras, as well as garden peas.

Pap's has a strong following, has won several awards and given a regular write-up in the *Jewish Chronicle*.

122

Fryer's Delight

19 Theobalds Road, Holborn, London WC1

Mon–Sat midday–10pm (restaurant); Mon–Sat midday–11pm (takeaway) • Busiest on Friday

B S skate and rock

The Fryer's Delight has been providing exceptional fare for about 32 years. Thanks to mentions in travel guides all over the world, the shop attracts an eclectic mix of customers, some of them drawn by reports that this is one of the best places in London to eat for under a fiver. About six minutes' walk from Holborn tube station, the shop is a simple affair. There are no frills, no

concessions to fads or fashion; the shop is exactly what it looks like from the outside.

Alongside your fish come thickly cut chips and a choice of mushy peas made in-house, monstrous pickles and wallies (pickled gherkins), and tartare sauce.

The Fryer's Delight has seen the likes of Trevor McDonald, Susannah York, Sterling Moss and many many more celebrity customers.

The Sea Shell

49–51 Lisson Grove, London NW1

Daily midday–2.30pm/5–10.30pm • Busiest on Friday

V **S** unless otherwise requested   BH Y iⓄi

A mere two minutes' walk from Marylebone Station – or a brisk stroll from Madame Tussaud's, The Planetarium and Lord's Cricket Ground – and round the corner from Regent's Park and the zoo, is one of the most efficient, attractive and best-thought-of fish and chip shops in London. The Sea Shell has an exclusive-looking restaurant and a traditional corner-shop takeaway.

The fish is delivered fresh every morning from Billingsgate Market and portioned into big pieces in the preparation area behind the gleaming chrome fryers. It is served with the skin on, unless you ask otherwise, boned and dipped in a standard batter mix that is beaten each morning and kept chilled (they also do a matzo-meal mix if requested). The fish is fried in groundnut oil at 177°C and emerges with a thick covering that is dry inside, even though the fish itself is beautifully succulent.

The reputation of this shop has extended worldwide and it has bee
visited by the Spice Girls, Michael Jackson, the Gallagher brothe

The menu lists a broad selection of fish – cod, haddock, skate, Dover sole, rock/huss, salmon, plaice on the bone, halibut, sea bass and rainbow trout – and you can have it grilled rather than fried if you prefer. Despite the extensive  choice, about 90 per cent of the customers prefer either cod or haddock with the medium-to-thick chips (freshly cut each day) and either mushy or garden peas, home-made coleslaw or home-made tartare sauce. If you choose to eat on the run, the shop provides a selection of recyclable cardboard cartons and paper bags.

For the most part, the customers are down-to-earth, being either local residents or office workers, regulars from other parts of London, or tourists and passing trade. But no matter who they are, they can expect to be treated in the same way and served with the same tasty fare.

nd Bernie Ecclestone (Formula One supremo), which must have een one hell of a party.

Fish Central

149–151 Central Street, Clerkenwell/Finsbury, London EC1
Mon–Sat 11am–2.30pm/4.45–11pm • Busiest on Friday evening

V **S**

BH ⛃ 🍽

Fish Central lies about halfway between Old Street and Farringdon tube stations in the tight little backstreets so redolent of Victorian London. Yet the buildings on Central Street are relatively modern, and the shopping square in which this fish shop resides was built in the mid-1960s.

George Hussein has owned the shop since 1968, but he has been buying and frying since 1955, and these days he tries to take a back seat to enable his son to learn the business. The shop is about to expand and by the time you read this, the airy restaurant should have doubled in size. The menu is freshly stocked every day with a choice of cod, haddock, plaice, skate (both whole and wings), rock/huss, halibut, monkfish, John Dory, queenfish and Dover sole. There are also some delightful home-made salmon fish cakes. The extensive menu allows

"When business is good, people eat fish and chips. When busine is bad, people eat fish and chips. Start a fish and chip shop ar

for the fact that prices for some fish (particularly cod) have gone through the roof as fish stocks have become endangered, so it is vital to offer alternatives in order to reduce the strain on fish populations and to provide an increasing diversity for the ever more demanding and refined English palate.

Most importantly, everything here is bought fresh from Billingsgate Market and the quality is tip-top. All the day's catches are served boneless and with the skin on, and are portioned with a very hungry customer in mind, before being dipped in a family batter recipe (though they'll do a matzo-meal batter if you ask), which produces a light golden, almost transparent coating. The fish and the thick chips are all fried in groundnut oil at around 180°C, unless you want grilled fish, and the food is wrapped in paper if you're eating alfresco – you'll find a few city benches around the area, but sadly little or no greenery.

"ou'll never go hungry." Warren Mitchell (actor and comedian), lias Alf Garnett.

North Sea Fish Restaurant

7–8 Leigh Street, St Pancras, London WC1
Mon–Sat midday–2.30pm/5.30–11pm (the restaurant closes 30 mins earlier) • Busiest on Friday

V **S** *S* Dover sole

About halfway between the tube stations of Kings Cross/St Pancras and Russell Square, is a fantastic eatery – the North Sea Fish Restaurant and Takeaway. It has been in the same hands for 27 years and is something of an institution. The custom consists of residents, workers, regulars from afar and tourists. The menu includes steamed fish and vegetables and a legendary array of desserts.

Cod is served with the skin on, as is haddock, plaice, skate, sea bass, plaice on the bone and trout, but they remove the skin from the Dover sole, which is scrumptious. All the fish is cooked to order, in a light crispy batter.

Great accompaniments are the traditional mushy peas, which have a smooth texture, and the home-made tartare sauce.

Faulkners

424–426 Kingsland Road, Kingsland, London E8
Daily at lunchtimes and evenings • Busiest on Friday and throughout the weekend

 🍽

About ten minutes' walk from Dalston Kingsland Railway Station is Faulkners. What's important here is the quality of the raw materials and each morning the folk from the shop are down at Billingsgate sniffing out the best fresh fish.

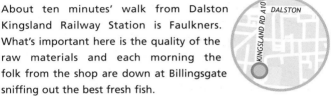

The menu is testament to the traditional roots of the shop, listing cod, rock/huss, skate, plaice, Dover sole, halibut, salmon, and both plaice and haddock on the bone. If you're

hungry and fancy something a bit different, try the plaice on the bone, which has a fresh flavour, and is colossal, like the halibut, which in turn gives your tastebuds a real kick.

the story goes, this is a fish and chip shop where lots of aces" meet up and tell old stories about the Krays.

Toff's

38 Muswell Hill Broadway, Muswell Hill, London N10
Mon–Sat 11.30am–11pm • Busiest in the evening, and all day on Friday

V **S** 🐟 tuna and swordfish   ⒝ℍ 🍷 🍽

Toff's gets its name from the original owners, the Tofali family. The current owners are George and Costas Georgiou. George used to be a customer and "liked it so much, he and his brother bought the company".

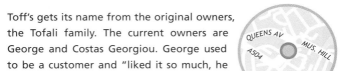

In a twist of the usual line of supply, the shop gets its fish from Grimsby before the rest of the Grimsby fish is delivered to Billingsgate Market. The fish is then portioned in sea-monster-sized slices (10oz is the smallest piece in the shop). The choice of fish is astounding – cod, haddock, plaice and plaice on the bone, rock, skate, lemon and Dover sole, halibut, sea bass, salmon, trout and turbot are all served with the skin on, while it is removed from the tuna and swordfish. The brothers, through their extensive menu and precise preparation, are determined that every customer will have a complete fish-eating experience to live long in the memory.

In 1999, radio DJ Zoë Ball officially launched the Fish & Chip Fan Clu taking the solemn oath, "I swear my allegiance to fish and chips …

Harbour Fish and Chip Shop

11–13 Salt Lane, Salisbury, Wiltshire
Mon 5–10pm, Tues–Sat 11.30am–2.15pm/5–10pm • Busiest on Tuesday, Friday and Saturday

This shop is run by an ex-polypropylene worker (Robert O'Keeffe), who used his redundancy money to fulfil a lifelong dream. He has built up a local following, yet also attracts people from further afield and plenty of tourists in the summer.

The fish selection here consists of cod, haddock, huss, skate and salmon, all coated in a thin and crunchy batter. The fish

comes from the deep waters of the North Atlantic. Robert also makes fish cakes, which are well worth a go if you're in the mood for something a bit different, and the chips are flash-fried to give them that extra crisp edge.

For alfresco eating, take a two-minute walk to the gardens of an old church that has been converted into an arts centre.

Trawlerman Fish & Chips

West Swindon Shopping Centre, Swindon, Wiltshire
Mon–Sat 11.15am–11pm • Busiest Thursday, Friday (particularly 4–6.30pm) and Saturday

This is one of only two fish and chip shops I have known to thrive in the middle of an out-of-town shopping centre. The reason the Trawlerman succeeds is because of the quality of its product and the fact that it caters predominantly to two different types of customer – the visiting shopper and the residents of the nearby housing development.

The Trawlerman is a clean and precise chippy that has

operated for 18 years, serving, in the main, Norwegian cod. Alternatives are haddock, plaice, skate and rock. They also serve excellent wallies (pickled gherkins) here.

The method here produces luscious white fish beneath crisp batter and thick chips that go well with the mushy peas

J. Henry's Fish & Chips

5 Upper Northam Road, Hedge End, Hampshire

Mon–Thurs 11.30am–2pm/5–11pm, Fri–Sat 11.30am–2pm/4.30–11pm, Sun 5–10pm • Busiest Friday

V **S**

Beyond the hustle and bustle of Southampton is a residential area called Hedge End. At its centre is J. Henry's, a community shop with two tables outside. In 1997, the shop was voted Fish and Chip Shop of the Year by the Sea Fish Industry Authority, which is no surprise, since they have been in the business for over 20 years. When the owners are not raising money for charity, they fry up a storm with Norwegian cod, haddock and plaice. All the fish

is served in portions of 6–10oz, covered in a light batter and served alongside stonking thick chips. Among the extras are pea fritters, which are mushy-like peas in a pattie coated with batter.

mong the visitors you might see here is Matt Le Tissier, ero of all Southampton football fans, who calls regularly.

Seafare

64 Normandy Street, Alton, Hampshire
Mon–Sat 11.30am–2pm/5–11pm, Sun 5–11pm • Busiest on Friday and Saturday

V S

It's worth going a few miles out of your way just to get some fish and chips from Seafare and, if it's raining, catching a movie at Alton's characterful cinema.

Duncan Nash has been operating here for about four years and has been in the business of fish-buying and frying for about 15 years. He has very definite ideas about what he wants, and the outcome is some excellent North Sea and North Atlantic cod, haddock, plaice and rock/huss, portioned generously and served boneless. The fish is fried in extremely hot palm oil, which produces a pale golden outer layer of batter containing moist, but not oily, pure white flesh. They operate a two-tier chip policy, using Maris Pipers or Sandy Farm new spuds, thus offering a choice of thickly cut (better for you) and thinly cut (don't retain heat or goodness).

if you stick around at Seafare you might spot famous gardener Alan Titchmarsh, who is a regular local customer

The Fat Friars

2 Hunter Avenue, Willesborough, Ashford, Kent

Mon 5–9pm, Tues–Sat 11.30am–2pm/5–9pm • Busiest on Thursday, Friday and Saturday

V | **$** except haddock

At first glance this tiny fish and chip shop may look unprepossessing, but it's a knockout. The shop had to be refurbished after a fire and they're back and better than ever.

Alf Phillips owns the place, his family having been in the business for nearly a hundred years, and he is a character from the larger-than-life mould. His personality and attention to detail are reflected in this dynamo of a chippy where you can get haddock, cod, skate, salmon, swordfish steaks, shark steaks, hoki (from New Zealand) and scallops in batter. Along with the standard accompaniments are creamed chervil and mussel chowder.

The shop boasts a shelfload of awards and has a reputation extending beyond the county's boundaries. Some customers drive many miles and have their orders specially wrapped in aluminium foil to keep them warm for the journey home.

Alf even has a customer as far away as Toronto in Canada, for whom he freezes orders of fish and chips and flies them out.

Newington Fish Bar

55b Newington Road, Ramsgate, Kent
Restaurant: Mon–Sat 11.30am–1.30pm/4.30–8pm Takeaway: Mon–Sat 11.30am–2pm/4.30–10.30pm

 except cod

This popular stretch of the Kent coastline is defined by grand Georgian architecture (contrasting with drab 1960s streets), long sandy beaches, cliff-top sea views and a busy harbour full of character. For a long time, Ramsgate and Margate have been favourite day-trip destinations of Cockneys and Essex boys and girls, so it always seems lively, particularly round the mother of all modern piers. Margate was once described

by Oscar Wilde as the "nom-de-plume of Ramsgate", suggesting there was little difference between the two places, but the area shows a good deal more character than it's given credit for.

**Owned by Mr Derrets, the Newington Fish Bar is a roadsid
business that has been in the same hands and on the sam**

The Newington Fish Bar is only a five-minute drive from the cliff seats, the seafront and the general hullabaloo of Ramsgate. Being set back a bit works to the shop's advantage, since they can quickly serve their regular snaking queues, and the food is fresh from the pan.

The fish is either Icelandic in origin or Norwegian from the North Atlantic. The cod is served skinless, while all the other fish – skate, haddock, plaice and rigg (also known as huss or rock) – keep their skin on. After being coated in a well-worked standard batter, the fish is then fried in sizzling palm oil, as are the standard-to-thick chips, before the whole meal is dished up in paper only. The proprietors make their own mushy peas and colourful curry sauce, listed with the usual side orders, as well as mushrooms and baked beans. This is a minimum-fuss operation with great-value food and is well worth the short trip inland away from the tourist flash.

spot for about 20 years. It is more of a community shop than a tourist stop-over, although naturally they happily serve anyone.

Butler's

12 Jengers Mead, Billingshurst, Sussex
Mon–Sat midday–2pm/5–10pm • Busiest at lunchtimes and all day Friday and Saturday

V **S** unless otherwise requested

Long-time servant to anybody passing through or near the village of Billingshurst, Butler's is found in a red-brick square. The shop has been in operation for six years and the family that owns it has been in the business for over 30. Currently, it's run by a friendly young husband-and-wife team. The standard portions of fish are a hearty 7–8oz, the menu consisting of cod,

haddock, plaice and rock/huss – all sourced from as far as the Icelandic and Norwegian fishing fleets. If you don't fancy sitting in your car to eat, prop yourself on one of the walls in the square and watch the world go by.

Here they do a special deal for elderly folk, promising a free portion of chips with fish bought between midday and 2pm

Mr Chips

32 Bishopric, Horsham, Sussex
Mon–Thurs midday–2.30pm/5–10pm, Fri–Sat till 10.30pm, Sunday 5–9pm • Busiest weekends

V 🐟 except haddock and skate

The town of Horsham is awash with cobbled and pedestrianized streets, which combine to make exploring it a pleasure.
On the menu at this shop you'll find cod, rock/huss, plaice, haddock and skate, all bought from the best of the North Atlantic catch. The fish is cut by hand into big pieces and served boneless (apart from the skate), and is accompanied by thick chips. Once armed with your tasty package, you have a choice

about where to eat. You can head to the nearby Bishopric Square, to sit among the ferns of a somewhat half-hearted tropical garden, or take a five-minute drive to the charms of Horsham Park.

heir attitude and why they are so good here is summed up
s: "Customers and staff are friends, and always friendly".

Harlees

94 Manor Road, Verwood, Dorset
Mon–Wed 11.30am–2pm/5–9pm; **Thurs–Sat** 11.30am–2.15pm/4.30–10pm; **Sun** 5–9pm • Busiest Fri-Sat

 except cod

The current proprietor of Harlees, Richard Long, is a great believer in professionalism, hygiene, staff and customer relations, and buying the best raw materials to produce the best product. The shop concentrates on supplying a mouth-watering product for its steadfast local customers and further-flung regulars alike.

The excellent cod, plaice, haddock and rock/huss are coated in

thin batter, cooked at high temperatures, then served with thick chips. Places to eat are limited to the car park or Potterne Recreation Ground, three minutes' walk away – a playing field with benches and a children's play area.

For many years, Buster Merrifield (Uncle Albert in *Only Fools and Horses*) was a regular customer here.

Fish 'n' Fritz

9 Market Street, Weymouth, Dorset
Daily midday–2pm/5–9pm (midday–9pm from Easter) • Busiest in summer

V **S** plaice and haddock **✗** cod and huss

Paul and Julie Hay have been on this site for four years. They have built up a strong local following with their cod, haddock, plaice and rock/huss, together with an extensive vegetarian menu (the pea fritters and vegetable schnitzels are popular choices).

In wet weather, takeaways can be consumed at the counter and, when it's fine, the beach and harbour beckon.

Celebrity visitors include summer-season stars such as Rose Royce, Vince Hill, Bobby Davro and Bonnie Langford. However, the most highly prized guest is fish guru Rick Stein, who listed the shop in his *Seafood Lovers' Guide*.

This shop was the 2001 winner of the Sea Fish Industry Authority "Fish Shop of the Year" award for the southwest.

Capel's of Exmouth and Brixington

Capel's of Exmouth, 11 Imperial Road, Exmouth, Devon
Easter–Sept, Mon–Sat 11.15am–10pm, Sun midday–8pm; rest of the year, Mon–Sat 11.15am–10pm

Capel's of Brixington, 41 Pines Road, Brixington, Exmouth, Devon
Mon–Sat midday–2pm/4.30–9pm • Busiest on Friday and Saturday (both shops)

Capel's of Exmouth 🍽️

Tim and Sue Bond own two fish shops in the glorious town of Exmouth, a Georgian seaside haunt that once boasted among its residents the wives of Nelson and Byron, who were near neighbours – geographically speaking, at least. This is undoubtedly a lovely spot with a two-mile beach and both shops are located just a touch inland. The first (Capel's of Exmouth) is in the best location, lying near the main drag of the town and a two-minute drive or ten-minute walk from the sea; the other (Capel's of Brixington) is tucked away in the red-brick anonymity of a fairly recent housing estate, about 15 minutes' drive from the seafront, but worth the trip.

Tim and Sue have been involved in the fish business for

The main aim of both shops is to provide an excellent and good-value meal for their regulars. Lucky for the visitors

142

17 years and serve an excellent product. At Capel's of Exmouth take your pick between cod, haddock, plaice or huss/rock, or special OAP

meals (a smaller piece of cod with bread and butter and a cup of tea). At Capel's of Brixington the menu extends to include not only cod, haddock, plaice and huss/rock but also red snapper (gorgeous), skate and lemon sole.

The fish for both shops comes from the Icelandic fleet and is served skinless and boneless, having been dipped in a secret

family batter recipe and fried with fairly chunky golden chips.

Any member of staff who isn't in the family has worked for the Bonds for so long that they might as well be.

really. The service here is efficient and friendly – you're pretty much guaranteed a smile with your supper.

Maddy's

25 St James's Place, Ilfracombe, Devon

Daily, May–Sept midday–11pm; Oct–Apr midday–10pm • Busy in summer & winter weekends

Ilfracombe is probably the most popular tourist stop-off on the north coast of Devon, as it has been since the Victorians and Edwardians started the fad for holidaying at seaside towns, so no wonder it contains many of the classic ingredients of an English resort.

On the classy side is Maddy's, its bright broad shopfront heralding excellent grub. Mark Maddison has worked in the business for 25 years, of which he has spent 15 at this spot. He's

a committed and friendly man who is fussy about his fish and buys his cod, haddock and plaice from the Icelandic fleet. Once it has been portioned by hand into hearty pieces and the skin and bones removed,

"Coming from a coastal town like Plymouth, I was brought up o fish and chips – we often used to pick them up on the way hom

the fish is dipped in a well-beaten standard batter that gives a light crispy finish, then fried in sizzling palm oil and served with thick chips. If you're looking for extras, the home-made mushy peas, in particular, are smooth and tasty.

As far as celebrity customers are concerned, the artist Damien Hirst comes here, as does Les Dennis, the gameshow host.

For those planning to take their food away, it is wrapped in polystyrene trays and paper, but anyone who wants paper only will be happily obliged. A five-minute walk in either direction along the promenade will bring you to a small crescent bay of golden sand where you can enjoy your meal.

from swimming training." Sharron Davies, former international swimming champion, author and broadcaster.

Squires

71 Torbay Road, Paignton, Devon
July–Sept, daily 10am–10.30pm; winter, daily 10am–7.30pm • Busiest Sunday lunchtime

3 Churston Broadway, Dartmouth Road, Churston, Paignton, Devon
Mon–Sat 10am–2pm/4.30–9pm • Busiest Friday

 except haddock

BH Both ⛘

Paignton is lucky enough to sport a couple of decent fish and chip shops, with the same name. The Torbay Road shop – hidden amongst the ice-cream parlours – is five minutes' walk from the seafront; the other is in a shopping district to the rear of the town.

Both shops handle Icelandic, Norwegian or Russian cod, haddock, lemon sole and rock, and Brixham skate, when it's available. The inland shop has won a variety of awards for food and hygiene.

 Ian Smith (Harold Bishop in *Neighbours*) has been to th[e] seaside shop, while Ray Reardon visits the inland restaurant

Kelly's

28 Fore Street, Saltash, Cornwall
Daily 10am–9pm • Busiest on Friday and Saturday at lunchtimes and 4–6.30pm

 🍽

For sustenance, the best place to go in Saltash is Kelly's, a family-run high-street fish shop that looks after the local community and welcomes weary travellers. The cod, haddock and plaice are the best fish available from the Arctic seas, where there's a predominance of pollution-free water. The fish is dipped in the family's own batter mix made up for them in the Midlands,

and fried in extremely hot palm oil. You'll be given a portion of hearty chips and whatever takes your fancy from extras, such as home-made mushy peas. Takeaway meals are dished up in boxes to keep them hot and fresh.

Kelly has owned the shop for four years, and has been involved in fish-frying for about 12, picking up 19 awards since 1988.

Harbour Lights

7–9 Arwenack Street, Falmouth, Cornwall
Daily 11am–midnight • Busiest at weekends

♉ 🍽

This shop has been in existence for 20 years and operated under the same management (Connie) for 15. The new owners, Peter Fraser and Simon Daw, have had the good sense to avoid tinkering too much with a winning formula.

The main demand is for cod and haddock from Iceland, followed by plaice, which are all coated in the shop's personalized batter and accompanied by thick chips. They

also make their own excellent fish cakes. They even offer changing facilities for mothers with babies or small children, which just goes to prove that they are prepared to go that little bit further.

Side orders include home-made mushy peas, a vegetable based curry sauce and cheesy chips or coleslaw.

Truscotts

19 Fore Street, Newquay, Cornwall

Daily, Easter–Oct 11.30am–11pm; rest of the year, midday–2pm/5–8pm • Busiest in summer

V **S** plaice **✗** cod and haddock

It's hard to imagine Newquay without the summer crowds in its tight streets, and even harder to imagine it without a buzzing fish and chip shop. The Truscotts have spent 32 years as a fish-frying family – Alan and Diane are the experienced and committed cooks, and 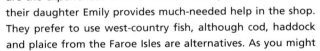 their daughter Emily provides much-needed help in the shop. They prefer to use west-country fish, although cod, haddock and plaice from the Faroe Isles are alternatives. As you might

expect, their batter mix is a tightly guarded secret that perfectly complements the fine fish. In addition to the fish and chips, you'll find a comprehensive list of side dishes here.

The Truscotts think of their shop as one that principally serves the locals and happens to benefit from a lively passing trade.

Fryer Tucks

Harlyn Road, St Merryn, just outside Padstow, Cornwall
Easter–Oct only: Mon–Sat 11.30am–2pm/5–9pm, Sun 5–9pm • Busiest Thursday, Friday, Saturday

St Merryn is a sparsely populated dot on a pretty landscape, only a short car journey from its larger, and better-known neighbour, Padstow – the principal fishing port on this coast made famous by TV chef Rick Stein. In light of this you might think Fryer Tucks would be so overshadowed as to have an inferiority complex, but not a bit of it. They have been going for the last 30 years and even had the temerity to expand (18 years ago) by opening a cafe-cum-fish-and-chip-shop called Quayside at

the harbour in Padstow. The buzzing St Merryn shop employs plenty of local staff and dishes up some wonderful fare. The fish is usually

A few of their many celebrity customers stand out, such a comedian Lenny Henry, actor Edward Woodward, BB

Icelandic – cod and plaice – portioned by hand and served boneless. They coat the fish in a well-worked standard batter that is cooked in hot groundnut oil and the thick chips (from Maris Piper or Wilja potatoes) are fried in a separate vegetable oil. For added extras you can try the mushy peas or vegetable-based curry sauce. Whether you're eating in the shop or taking away, the price is the same. If you're heading for the beach, about four minutes' drive away, you can have the food put on trays and wrapped in paper; alternatively you can eat in their modern, medium-sized restaurant or take your pick of one of the many tables and benches outside the front of the shop.

Holiday presenter Sanka Guha and 1960s pop star Frank Ifield of *I Remember You* fame).

The Mermaid

11 Belle Vue Lane, Bude, Cornwall

Whitsun–Sept, Mon–Sat 11.45–2pm/4.45–9pm; rest of the year, Tues–Sat 11.45am–2pm/4.45–8pm

B **V** mixture 🏷   **BH**

Bude is Cornwall's most northerly town, surrounded by towering and moody cliffs near the Devon border and built beside a river estuary. It's popular with surfers and kayakers, but has never been one of the really big tourist attractions, so it makes an excellent place to visit to enjoy hot food in relatively uncrowded surroundings. The best place is Summerleaze Beach, a broad stretch of windswept golden sand just a two-minute drive or five-minute walk from The Mermaid, which is in the centre of this neat little town.

Malcolm and Jane Jarvis have been running the shop for nine years, although the extended family has worked in fish-frying for about 30. They prefer Icelandic or Norwegian cod, haddock and plaice, which they cut by hand into big portions, serve skinless and boneless, and coat in a thin crisp batter. The frying

The assertion that this is a community shop is born out by the fa that the majority of the customers are locals, for whom they ope

takes place at a high temperature (at least 180°C) in a mixture of vegetable oil and beef dripping, which is changed every three days. Their chips are a standard size, usually made from either Maris Piper or Wilja potatoes, and they offer excellent battered pea fritters as well as a lively curry sauce.

Tucked away on a narrow road in the centre of town, The Mermaid is no doubt missed by a few unsuspecting tourists, but anyone in the town will soon point you in the right direction.

ll year round, and they tend to be only slightly less busy in the winter months than during the tourist season.

Seafish Award-Winning Shops

AVON

Clock Tower Fisheries
84 Regent Street, Kingswood, Bristol

Farrow's Fish and Chips
Unit 8, Kingsway Shopping Precinct,
Bristol

The Frying Machine
Brook Way, Bradley, Stoke, Bristol

BERKSHIRE

Dorothy's Fish and Chip Shop
8 The Square, Harmanswater, Bracknell

Sanders
158 Park Lane, Tilehurst, Reading

BUCKINGHAMSHIRE

Napoli Fish Bar
175 Newport Road, New Bradwell,
Milton Keynes

Napoli Fenny Fish Bar
86 Aylesbury Street, Fenny Stratford,
Milton Keynes

Smiles Fish and Chips
4 The Broadway, Penn Road, Beaconsfield

CAMBRIDGESHIRE

Eaton Plaice
66 St Neots Road, Eaton Ford, St Neots

CHESHIRE

Les's Fish Bar
51 Victoria Street, Crewe

Jackson's Supper Bar
24a Church Street, Wilmslow

Derby Fish Bar
3 Derby Way, Marple, Stockport

The Dolphin
592 Gorton Road, Nr Reddish, Stockport

Horatio's
163 Gilbent Road, Cheadle Hulme

Rob's Fish & Chip Bar
74 Warmingham Lane, Middlewich

Les's Fish Bar
15 Dingle Walk, Winsford, Cheshire

Poynton Fish Bar
49 London Road South, Poynton

Ladybrook Fish Bar
12 Fir Road, Bramhall, Cheshire

CLEVELAND

Barnacles
113-115 Linthorpe Road, Middlesbrough

Oxbridge Fish Bar
50 Oxbridge Lane, Oxbridge,
Stockton on Tees

Russell's Fish and Chip Restaurant
7-18 Bath Street, Redcar

Coulby Newham Fish Bar
Unit 1 Site K, Parkway Centre, Coulby,
Newham, Middlesbrough

Barnacles
146 Queensway, Billingham

Mariners
39 Middleton Grange Centre, Hartlepool

Hartburn Fish Bar
Harper Parade, Darlington Road,
Hartburn, Stockton

Seabreeze Fish & Chips
27, The Wynd, Marske by the Sea, Redcar

The Flighty Cod,
105 High Street, Yarm

Croft Avenue Fisheries
37 Croft Avenue, Acklam, Middlesbrough

Hutton Lane Fish Shop
2 Esk Close, Guisborough

COUNTY DURHAM

Rise Carr Fish Bar
224 Whessoe Road, Darlington

Steps Fish Restaurant
1 Upper Yoden Way, Peterlee Town Centre, Peterlee

Bell's Fish Shop
33 Marshall Terrace, Gilesgate Moor, Durham

Morleys
12 Fore Bondgate, Bishop Auckland

Beedles Chippy
2 Oaklea Terrace, Cockerton Hill Road, Bishop Auckland

Johnson's Traditional Fish & Chips
39 Front Street, Sacriston

Atlantis Fast Food
110 Whitby Way, Darlington

CORNWALL

Fryer Tucks
St Merryn, Harlyn Road, Padstow

Quayside Café
17 N Quay, Padstow

Hutchinson's Fish & Chips
95 Meneage Street, Helston

Your Plaice Or Mine
8 Victoria Road, Camelford

Truscotts
19 Fore Street, Newquay

Kelly's
28 Fore Street, Saltash

Holmbush Fish Bar
86 Daniels Lane, Holmbush, St Austell

Sole Plaice
20 Pydar Street, Truro

Beacon Fish & Chips Bar
72 Fore Street, Beacon, Camborne

Harbour Lights
Arwenack Street, Falmouth

Kellys of Looe
Fore Street, East Looe

CUMBRIA

Matties
186 Ainslie Street, Barrow in Furness

Stramongate Chip Shop
74 Stramongate, Kendal

The Esk Café
4 English Street, Longtown

Town Head Chippy
46 Stricklandgate, Penrith

DERBYSHIRE

Steve's Fish Bar
1250 London Road, Alvaston

The Frying Squad
125 Oaklands Avenue, Littleover, Derby

The Coach House
3 Scarsdale Place, High Street, Buxton

DEVON

Polsloe Bridge Fish & Chips
191 Pinhoe Road, Whipton, Exeter

Squires Fish Restaurant
Exeter Road, Braunton

Bloaters of Sidford
8 Church Street, Sidford, Sidmouth

The Whiddon Fryer
1 Coppice Close, Westacott Road, Barnstaple

Hanburys Licensed Fish Restaurant
Princes Street, Babbacombe, Torquay

Capels of Brixington
41 Pines Road, Brixington, Nr. Exmouth

The Jolly Good Fish Café
6 Teign Street, Teignmouth

Capels of Exmouth
11 Imperial Road, Exmouth

Squires Restaurant & Takeaway
3 Churston Broadway, Dartmouth Road, Churston, Paignton

Squires of Paignton
71 Torbay Road, Paignton

DORSET

Fish 'n' Fritz
9 Market Street, Weymouth

All-ways Fridays
251 Blandford Road, Hamworthy Poole

Daniels
159 Abbotsbury Road, Weymouth

Harlees Fish & Chips
159 Wareham Road, Corfe Mullen, Poole

Case & Brewer
1 Victoria Road, Dorchester

Harlees
94 Manor Road, Verwood

EAST SUSSEX

Trident Fish Restaurant
23 Albert Parade, Green Street, Old Town, Eastbourne

Peters Fish Bar
25 London Road, Bexhill on Sea

EAST YORKSHIRE

Golden Fry
41 Saville Street, Hull

Larry's Fish Bar
53 Saville Street, Hull

ESSEX

Reg's
70 Ravensdale, Gt. Clacton

GLOUCESTERSHIRE

The Frying Machine
26a High Street, Thornbury

Mike Brutons Fish & Chips
8 North Street, Winchcombe

GREATER MANCHESTER

Parade Fish Bar
3 The Parade, The Precinct, Swinton, Trafford Park, Manchester

Langley Friery
227 Wood Street, Middleton

Tony's Chippy
3 Percy Street, Ancoats, Manchester

Compo's of Oldham
270 Manchester Street, Oldham

HAMPSHIRE

Seafare
64 Normandy Street, Alton

Trawlerman
Chineham Shopping Centre, Basingstoke

The Codfather
6 Botley Road, Hedge End, Southampton

J. Henry's Fish & Chips
5 Upper Northam Road, Hedge End, Southampton

HERTFORDSHIRE

Wrights
3 East Street, Ware

Skippers
50 The Common, Hatfield

KENT

The Fat Friars
2 Hunter Avenue, Willesborough, Ashford

Newington Fish Bar
55b Newington Road, Ramsgate

LANCASHIRE

Pisces
92 Poulton Road, Fleetwood

Belfields
72 Parliament Street, Burnley

St Annes Fish Restaurant
41 St Andrews Road, Lytham St Annes

Seafarers
341-343 Cliffton Drive South, St Annes

York Street Chippy
2 York Street, Accrington

Fishers Plaice
29 Westcliffe Drive, Layton, Blackpool

Seniors
106 Normoss Road, Blackpool

The Fishery
273 Devonshire Road, Blackpool

Holloways Fish & Chips
2 Towneley Street, Burnley

Andy's Fish & Chips
55 Marlborough Road, Accrington

The Friendly Fryer
86 Hindle Street, Darwen

Joyces Plaice
21 Shakespeare Road, Fleetwood

Musketts Traditional Fish & Chips
19 Market Street, Leigh

Hodgson's Chippy
96 Prospect Street, Lancaster

Frying Squad
110 Lytham Road, Blackpool

Cemetery Chippy
75 Keighley Road, Colne

Tim's Chip Stop
604 Bacup Road, Waterfoot, Rossendale

Mere Park Fisheries
252 Preston Old Road, Blackpool

LEICESTERSHIRE

Roxy Chippy
300 Fosse Road South, Leicester

LINCOLNSHIRE

Avenue Fish and Chips
9 Rycroft Avenue, Deeping St James

Great Barrier Reef
Highfield House, Princess Margaret
Avenue, Metheringham

Linfords Traditional Fish 'N' Chips
6 Market Place, Market Deeping

BJ's Quality Fish & Chips
127 West Street, Alford

Mr Chips of Louth
17/21 Aswell Street, Louth

Sea Lane Fisheries
206 North Sea Lane, Humberston, Grimsby

Turners Fish Restaurant
20 Red Lion Street, Spalding

LONDON

Pap's Fish Restaurant
23 The Broadway, Southgate, London

Bab's Fish Bar
561 High Road, Tottenham, London

Olley's Traditional Fish & Chips
69 Norwood Road, Herne Hill, London

MERSEYSIDE

Mr. Chips
5 Preston New Road, Churchtown,
Southport

Mikes Fish & Chips
75 Churchill Avenue, Southport

MIDDLESEX

Cowley Fish Bar
28 High Road, Cowley, Uxbridge

NORFOLK

Daves Fish Restaurant
7–11 Co-Operative Street, Sheringham

Moby Dicks
1 Black Horse Road, Clenchwarton,
Kings Lynn

Quayside Chippy
The Quay, Wells Next The Sea

French's Fish Shop
10 Quayside, Wells-next-the-Sea

NORTHAMPTONSHIRE

Rafferty's
67 Occupation Road, Corby

NORTHUMBERLAND

Harbour Fish Bar
1 Broomhill Street, Amble, Morpeth

Fryer's Plaice
48 Preistpopple, Hexham

Balls of Prudhoe
39 Front Street, Prudhoe

Robert Smith's Quality Takeaway
190 Main Street, Tweedmouth

Charlies
Albert Street, Amble, Morpeth

NORTH YORKSHIRE

Mr C's
61-63 Micklegate, Selby

Millers
55 The Village, Haxby, York

Robertson's Fish Restaurant & Chips Away
6-7 Bridge Street, Whitby

The Magpie Café
14 Pier Road, Whitby

Lead Lane Fisheries
27-29 Lead Lane, Ripon

Dougies Fish& Chips
66 King Edwards Drive, Harrogate

Royal Fisheries
48 Baxtergate, Whitby

Bizzie Lizzies
36 Swadford Street, Skipton

Mister Chips
68–69 Church Street, Whitby

Barkers of Richmond
14 Pier Road, Whitby

Strensall Fisheries
16 The Village, Strensall, York

Ingham's Fish Restaurant
40 Belle Vue Street, Filey

Quarterdeck Restaurant
Pier Road, Battery Parade, Whitby

Newmarket Fisheries
50 Newmarket Street, Skipton

Thompson's Traditional Fish & Chips
8 Main Street, Stamford Bridge, York

Quayside
7 Pier Road, Whitby

NOTTINGHAMSHIRE

Andys Fish Bar
89 Bracebridge Drive, Bilborough

Georgio's Plaice
195 Sneinton Dale, Nottingham

RUTLAND

Silver Fish
3 North Street East, Uppingham

SHROPSHIRE

Wot's Cookin
24 Willow Street, Oswestry

SOMERSET

The Cod Father
Unit 3, Clover Court, Locking Castle, Weston-Super-Mare

Knight's Fish Restaurant
5 Northload Street, Glastonbury

Morgans
49/51 Hamilton Road, Taunton

SOUTH YORKSHIRE

Harbour Lights
50-52 High Street, Epworth, Doncaster

Lonsdale Fisheries
41 Sandringham Road, Intake, Doncaster

Robert's Golden Cod
21 Church Street, Armthorpe, Doncaster

Robert's Golden Cod
8 High Street, Epworth, Doncaster

Stephen's Orginal Golden Cod
231 Beckett Road, Wheatley, Doncaster

Dale Road Fish Bar
1 Dale Road, Rawmarsh, Rotherham

Shaws Fish & Chip Shop
337 Pontefract Road, Lundwood, Barnsley

STAFFORDSHIRE

Mr Chips
31 High Street, Kinver

Kinver Chippery
122a High Street, Kinver

SUFFOLK

Bounty Fisheries
115 High Road West, Felixstowe

SURREY

Henry Higgins
2 Linkfield Corner, Redhill

Seafare
147 Worplesdon Road, Guildford

Seafare Fish & Chips
104a Hermitage Road, St Johns, Woking

Seafare
206 London Road, Burpham, Guildford

Skippers
10 Upper Green West, Mitcham

Mr Chips
344 Hook Road, Chessington

Mr Chips
215 Chipstead Valley Road, Coulsdon

Seafare
7-8 Bridge Street, Godalming

TYNE & WEAR

Porcelli's Fish & Chips
7 Valley Shopping Parade, Kingsway North, Team Valley Trading Estate, Gateshead

Golden Fry Inn
85 Station Avenue North, Fence Houses, Houghton Le Spring

Gill's Fish & Chips
53 West Percy Street, North Shields

Marshalls
33 Front Street, Tynemouth

Robson's Takeaway
57 Ravensworth Road, Dunston, Gateshead

Jarrow Mega Bite
52 Staple Road, Jarrow

Soave's
95 Edinburgh Road, Jarrow

WARWICKSHIRE

Heathcote Fish Bar
86 Heathcote Road, Whitnash, Leamington Spa

Hillmorton Fish Saloon
68 Featherbed Lane, Hillmorton, Rugby

Brownsover Fish Bar
124-126 Hollowell Way, Rugby

WEST MIDLANDS

Wollaston FishBar
101 Bridgnorth Road, Wollaston, Stourbridge

Broad Lane Chippy
303 Broad Lane, Kingsheath, Birmingham

Brockmoor Fryer
45 High Street, Brockmoor, Brierly Hill

Broadway Chippy
8 Hawes Close, Broadway, Walsall

The Blue Submarine
7 Middlepark Road, Russells Hall, Dudley

Stallings Fryer
Unit 5, Shop 11, Stallings Lane, Kingswinford

Victoria Chippy
10 Owen Street, Tipton

Hamstead Fish Bar
40 Old Walsall Road, Great Barr, B'ham

Reed Square
1010 Chester Road, Erdington, B'ham

Aldridge Fish Bar
27 Anchor Road, Aldridge, Walsall

WEST SUSSEX

Mr Chips
15 Langley Green Parade, Crawley

Blunden's
1 John Street, Shoreham by Sea

Butlers
12 Jéngers Mead, Billingshurst

Mr Chips
32 Bishopric, Horsham

WEST YORKSHIRE

The Cove Bridge Street Fisheries
17 Bridge Street, Otley

Websters of Baildon
39 Northgate, Baildon

Mugatroyds
Harrogate Road, Yeadon, Leeds

Bryans of Headingley
9 Weetwood Lane, Headingley, Leeds

Vicker Street Fisheries
134 High Street, Castleford

GJ's Takeaway
59a Holmsley Field Lane, Oulton, Leeds

Westfield Fisheries
5 New Road, Yeadon, Leeds

Harbour Lights
15 Leeds Road, Ilkley

Bretts Fish Restaurant
12 North Lane, Headingley, Leeds

Status Fisheries
2 Lindley Road, Bradford

Nashs Fish Restaurant
102 Harrogate Road, Chapel Allerton, Leeds

Wi'bits
941 Leeds Road, Huddersfield

Kingfisher
597 Denby Dale Road, Calder Grove, Wakefield

Maypole Fisheries
28 Cross Green, Otley

Wi'bits
83 Huddersfield Road, Mirfield

WILTSHIRE

Trawlerman
West Swindon Shopping Centre, Swindon

Bulford Fish & Chip Shop
9 Meadow Road, Bulford, Salisbury

Superfry
470 Ferndale Road, Swindon

Harbour Fish & Chips
11-13 Salt Lane, Salisbury

WORCESTERSHIRE

Foleys Fish Bar
Stourport Road, Kidderminster

Catchems End Fish Bar
134 Kidderminster Road, Bewdley

Lyppards Fryer
Unit 6 Lyppards Centre, Ankerage Green, Warndon Villages, Worcester

Merchants Fish Bar Restaurant
78–80 Load Street, Bewdley

Winyates Chippy
Unit 4 Winyates Centre, Redditch

Batchley Road Fish Bar
207 Batchley Road, Batchley, Redditch

Rainbow Hill Chippy
24 Ashwood Road, Rainbow Hill, Worcester

ACKNOWLEDGEMENTS

Tony Mudd would like to thank Laura Harper for both editorial input and encouragement; Jane Baldock for editing and overseeing the project; also all the people out there who recommended their favourite fish and chip shops by radio or by letter (and all those who will contribute to the next edition); and Mandy Lunn and Damien Moore for having the faith to back the idea in the first place.

Studio Cactus would like to thank David Ashby for creating the maps, John Sturges for proofreading, and Laura Seber and Aaron Brown for their editorial assistance. A special thank you to Sharon Moore for designing the book.

Picture Credits
Corbis: 10, 16; Hulton Getty: 9, 13, 14; Stockbyte: Front jacket, 6